CATCHING A FEA[...]
A Zen Retreat with Mas[...]

MW01067795

John Crook is Reader in Ethology (Animal Behaviour) at the Psychology Department of the University of Bristol. He first became interested in Buddhism when he was posted as a National Service army officer to Hong Kong in 1953–4. In recent years he has studied both Tibetan Buddhism and Zen, visiting Ladakh, Hong Kong and Taiwan. He trains with Master Sheng Yen on Ch'an retreats in New York. In 1980 he published *The Evolution of Human Consciousness* (Oxford University Press), a synthesis of evolutionary biology, western and Buddhist psychology. In 1990, together with David Fontana, he edited and contributed to *Space in Mind: East–West Psychology and Contemporary Buddhism* (Element Books). He leads a retreat programme at a small house in the Welsh hills.

Ming Yee Wang is a computer consultant in Manhattan, New York, who has interpreted for Master Sheng Yen for many years.

Master Sheng Yen

CATCHING
A FEATHER
ON A FAN

A Zen Retreat with
Master Sheng Yen

Interpreter:
Ming Yee Wang

*Edited with an Introduction
and Commentaries by*
JOHN CROOK

ELEMENT BOOKS

First published in Great Britain in 1991 by
Element Books Limited
Longmead, Shaftesbury, Dorset

Cover photograph by Carole Bruce
Cover design by Max Fairbrother
Designed by Roger Lightfoot

Typeset by Footnote Graphics, Warminster, Wiltshire
Printed and bound in Great Britain by
Billings Ltd, Hylton Road, Worcester

British Library Cataloguing in Publication Data
Yen, Sheng
    Catching a feather on a fan : a zen retreat with Master
Sheng Yen.
1. Zen Buddhist life. Meditation
I. Title   II. Crook, John *1943*–
294.3443

ISBN 1–85230–194–5

}

To all practitioners
seeking to develop a
sure-footed Zen in
the West

CONTENTS

PREFACE

THERE ARE few full accounts of the proceedings of a Zen retreat. While a number of works provide excerpts from interviews with masters, details of procedure and ritual practices, only two books, so far as I know, take the reader through the whole process, thereby revealing the close interdependence of sitting, ritual, formal teaching and interviews. Both of these describe Ch'an (Chinese Zen) retreats. The first is Lu K'uan Yu's[1] translations of the daily lectures given by the great Master Hsu-yun at two week-long retreats at the Jade Buddha Monastery at Shanghai in 1953 which include some information about the events themselves. The second is an account of a seven day period of intensive Ch'an training given by Master Nan Huai-chin at Yang Ming Shan, Peitou, Taiwan in 1962. This account,[2] translated by Margaret Yuan and Janis Walker, is full of details regarding the events, participants' responses to the Master and the Master's own discourses and interjections. On both occasions the participants were Chinese and the retreats were conducted in that language.

This book provides thorough details of a Ch'an retreat led in Britain for British people (and one Chinese) by Master Sheng Yen of the Institutes of Chung-Hwa Buddhist Culture, Taipei and New York in 1989. The event arose following my own experiences with him at retreats in New York; and from my wish that friends who had participated in Western Zen retreats with me at my retreat house, Maenllwyd, in Wales could also have the opportunity of working with him. I am deeply grateful to Shih-fu for having responded so generously to my invitation.

The event and the Master's particular methods are described together with edited versions of all the talks, short and long, given during our time together. Master Sheng Yen gave these talks in Mandarin. They were ably interpreted on the spot by Ming Yee Wang. It is these interpretations that form the basis for my rendering. In a feature much favoured by Master Sheng Yen,[3] we also solicited detailed reports of the retreat participants' experiences and a number of these are presented here. This enables the reader to get the feel of a Ch'an retreat, its challenges, difficulties and opportunities, not only from the Master's presentation but also from the participants' responses. I have also included some stories and an autobiographical interview arising from a few days spent with Shih-fu in London after the retreat.

The book is the result of a suggestion from Master Sheng Yen that I prepare the taped talks for publication and set them in book form. Master Sheng Yen remarked that, since he was unlikely to return to Britain for some time, he had spoken to us more fully than is his usual practice in retreat. I gratefully acknowledge the help provided me by several members of the Ch'an Center at Elmhurst, New York, especially the critical readings by Ming Yee Wang and conversations with Dan Stevenson of Butler University, USA. Chris Marano combed through the text with an exemplary diligence rooting out ineffective expressions, tidying the punctuation and improving the phrasing. His understanding of the dynamics of English prose has contributed greatly to this book. Master Sheng Yen has of course been consulted throughout the preparation of the text and gave encouragement when doubts assailed me. Having fulfilled my task, it is now a pleasure to present this work to the public dedicating it to all who seek truth.

JHC

NOTES

1. Lu K'uan Yu, 1960, *Ch'an and Zen Teaching. First series*, (Century, London)
2. M. Yuan, and J. Walker, 1986, *Grass Mountain. A Seven day Intensive in Ch'an training with Master Nan Huai Chin*, (Samuel Weiser Inc, York Beach, Maine).
3. For examples see Sheng Yen, Master, 1982, *Getting the Buddha Mind: On the practice of Ch'an retreat*, (Dharma Drum, New York) and most numbers of the *Ch'an Magazine* published quarterly by the Institute of Chung Hwa Buddhist Culture, 90–56 Corona Avenue, Elmhurst, New York, 11373. Tel: (718) 592–6593.

INTRODUCTION

WALES WAS doing what it knows best; the rain was pelting down into a dark night, the farmside stream was rushing tumultuously down hill and the ash twigs lashed together above the house. Indoors a fire crackled in the hearth and the first arrivals for the retreat were finding their way damply to bed places in attics and a neighbouring barn. Suddenly a cry went up 'He's here!'

A battered Volkswagen van had pulled up in the muddy yard and, as I opened the front door, a very tired Ch'an Master was getting a shoe full of water as he stepped out. He had just completed some fifty hours of airtravel and the long drive from Heathrow Airport to reach us. Although extremely tired, he warmed up in front of the fire, inspected his accommodation and the house and quickly began to appreciate the company. Within an hour he had grasped the reins and begun the first Ch'an retreat led by a Master at the Maenllwyd.

I had first heard of Master Sheng Yen during a visit to Hong Kong in 1985 to pay my respects to my original teacher in Zen, Shih Yen Why, the director of Po Lin monastery on Lan Tao Island. Although I had several marvellous last meetings with him, it was clear that due to his age and deafness, he was at the end of his teaching career. It seemed important to begin the search for a younger master from whom I could receive guidance. I was visiting a Buddhist book shop down town when I came across a copy of *Getting the Buddha Mind*; indeed I could hardly avoid it since it was the only title in English. I much enjoyed reading this work and I realised that rather than searching around in the Far East, it would be easier to cross the Atlantic to sit with Master Sheng Yen in his New York centre. After I had attended two week-long retreats with him and enjoyed several lengthy and highly constructive conversations, he kindly consented to come to Britain to run a retreat for those who for some years had been pursuing the Dharma with me in 'Western Zen' retreats at my small Welsh farmhouse. Visa problems intervened and the first attempt was a failure; this was his second attempt and once again visa difficulties were nearly responsible for a last minute disaster. Indeed, most of the participants did not know on arrival whether he would be coming or not.

This book consists primarily of the twenty talks that Master Sheng Yen delivered to us on different occasions during the ensuing retreat. When the retreat closed, he requested that I prepare a book out of these recorded talks because he had given us a much more detailed presentation than was usual on such events. He told us it would not be easy for him to come again. So he had 'unpacked his bags and let us view all his wares'. In fulfilling this task I have there- fore had the pleasure of receiving his instruction many times over as I wrestled with problems of presentation.

Master Sheng Yen, or, to give him his full name, The Venerable Dr Chang Sheng Yen, is director of the Institute of Chung Hwa Buddhist Culture in Taipei, Taiwan and presi- dent of a similarly named institute in New York, which also runs the Ch'an Meditation Center, of which he is the master. Master Sheng Yen is also Abbot of a monastery in Taipei and a professor in the philosophy department of the University of Soo Chow. A brief autobiographical interview is provided at the end of this book.

A Ch'an master is known to his trainees as Shih-fu, a term

equivalent to the better-known Japanese word, Roshi. The term may also be used as a noun meaning a personal teacher. I shall refer to Master Sheng Yen as Shih-fu throughout most of this text. In order to present us with an orthodox retreat, Shih-fu brought with him Guo Yuen Shih, a monk in residence at the Ch'an Center, New York, who acted as organiser, disciplinarian and leader of chant (a man whose kindly charm won all our hearts) and an interpreter, Ming Yee Wang, whose skills in rendering long passages of speech with eloquence, precision and wit earned him our profound admiration. The 'team', as we called them, certainly fielded a strong side and it was up to us practitioners to match them with our responsiveness. In that Shih-fu taught us so thoroughly, I feel we did not entirely fail to rise to the occasion. I myself acted as guestmaster.

THE RETREAT

A Ch'an retreat is a period of intensive training that usually lasts seven days. The daily schedule was rigorous. Boards were hit at 4 am for a speedy rise leading to an assembly for physical exercises at 4.15 am. At this time, Shih-fu spoke briefly to give us a number of highly useful perspectives for the day. There were then three sitting periods each of half-hour duration before the morning liturgy was chanted. Breakfast followed in the same silence that characterised the whole event. After breakfast there was an hour's work period for which each participant had been allocated a job: washing-up, cleaning, bringing in logs, replacing candles (for we have no electricity) and filling paraffin stoves. After work, one or two people would steal a few minutes' rest, but this was not on the programme. Officially it was back to voluntary meditation or walking meditatively. Work period over, there followed five sitting periods between which, except for the last two, there were periods of standing yoga, sitting yoga, slow and fast walking. Since the house is small, the walking and running went on in a circle around the centre of a nearby field – much to the amusement of our local sheep farmer friend. After lunch and another work period there were a further five sittings with similar breaks until the evening chant of the Meng-shan offering (p. 13). Supper followed and then a period for washing and rest before the talk by the Master at about 7 pm. The day ended with three further sits, without break for exercises – simply a stretch or a brief massage. At 10 pm it was bed time, unless one wished to sit further into the night. Apart from interviews with Shih-fu, no talking between participants is allowed at any time.

Needless to say this gruelling schedule is a severe test for each participant's determination, ability to endure physical and mental pain, and capacity to resist fatigue. Why anyone should attempt it only becomes apparent after the first several days are over – even for those who have completed similar retreats before! Only one special dispensation was allowed us; tea and cake in the afternoon, a genuflection to a Maenllwyd tradition.

A Ch'an retreat is perhaps less well known in the West than its Japanese equivalent, the Zen Sesshin. It is therefore appropriate to provide some notes on the contrast between these two forms of Buddhist training. The differences between them are a reflection of the contrasting histories of the Zen tradition in the two countries and doubtless also of the cultural temperament of two civilisations. Both terms, Ch'an and Zen, derive from mispronunciations of the original Sanskrit word, Dhyana, which simply means meditation. Ch'an and Zen derive therefore from the same root, the Dhyana sect, whose doctrines first reached Chinese shores with the arrival of the legendary Bodhidharma in the sixth century CE. The particularity of this sect was its emphasis on the fundamental importance of meditation as the direct approach to an understanding of the Buddha Dharma. The famous verse which beautifully encapsulates this emphasis reads:

> A special transmission outside the scriptures
> No dependence upon words or letters
> Direct pointing to the soul of man
> Seeing into one's own nature.

The emphasis throughout the long history of Ch'an in both China and Japan was therefore always upon meditational practice rather than upon intellectual knowledge or devotional exercise. The aim is to recapture the Buddha's own experience under the Bodhi tree. Yet the manner and method of this practice varied; and sectarian differences, often surprisingly loudly argued, have stressed different ways of proceeding within the same fundamental view.

When Ch'an was transmitted to Japan from China the sectarian divide between the Lin-chi (J:Rinzai) and Ts'ao-tung (J:Soto) sects with their respective methods of meditation was well established. Hence we have come to associate Rinzai with koan (*kung-an*) practice and Soto with Shikantaza, or 'just sitting' facing a wall. Subsequently, however, Buddhism in China went through a period of severe decline during which many sects disappeared and the doctrine fell into disrepute.[1] Ch'an survived better than most other sects but in such small units and numbers that surviving groups tended to support each other with a resulting amalgamation of methods and practices.

When the great Ch'an Master Hsu-yun restored both monasteries and practice in the first half of the century, thus giving Buddhism a new life in China, the methods he taught were derived from the Lin-chi tradition with a liberal dose of Pure Land Buddhism as well. This eclectic approach, far from weakening Ch'an in China, gave it a width and flexibility which it retains, and makes it particularly valuable in the West.

Whereas in Japan young men had to be trained quickly in order to inherit the temples of their fathers, in China this pressure was latterly much less in evidence. The need to induce an initial enlightenment experience (*kensho*) in young Japanese priests before they could be considered qualified as temple occupants led to a system of schooling that emphasised harshness and a sort of Zen militarism that is not apparent in Ch'an. Strict as Ch'an is, there is a vein of humanism here that sometimes seems lacking in Japanese methods with their stress on Dharma heroism.

The argumentative relations that have often arisen between

the different Ch'an sects and which tend to crop up even today are not based on matters of substance. Both the main sects take their viewpoint from the Prajnaparamita literature of India which is largely interpreted according to the Tathagatagarbha doctrine.[2] The differences concern methods of practice and the mode of enlightenment, whereby 'seeing the nature' (kensho) comes into view. In fact, modern Japanese Zen is itself largely based on an eclectic fusion of Rinzai and Soto methods created by Harada Roshi, a Soto teacher, who had also studied koan under Rinzai masters. This approach was brought to America by Yasutani Roshi, who, like his master, emphasised the importance of an initial kensho. The Soto tradition of Dogen, by contrast, stresses that practice itself, when rightly understood, is itself enlightenment. This emphasis was brought to the USA by both Shunryu Suzuki Roshi and Jiyu Kennett Roshi. In Britain, Throssle Hole Priory in Northumberland, founded by Kennett Roshi, stresses Dogen's Soto, while the Zen Centre in London, founded by Dr Irmgard Schloegel (Ven Myokyo-ni) emphasises the Rinzai approach. Trainees in both traditions should recall Yasutani Roshi's opinion that 'Rinzai and Soto have their respective strong and weak points, but, since strong points are liable to change into weak points and evils, by correctly learning each kind of Zen the strong points of both are taken in ... each (teacher) may devise his characteristic methods of guidance without imitating anyone, in accordance with the times and adapting to the country'.[3] Chinese Ch'an, in its own way, has come to a very similar viewpoint and sustains a notably broad range of practices.

THE VIEW

Shih-fu is a second generation descendant in the lineage of Master Hsu-yun and has inherited the latter's broad approach. He has received transmissions from within the lineages of both the Ts'ao-tung and the Lin-chi traditions. Furthermore, having trained in Japan, where he received a doctorate in Buddhist literature, he is thoroughly familiar with Japanese approaches. His first emphasis is upon neither the koan nor upon 'just sitting' but rather upon counting the breath with awareness. Later, in interview, he negotiates a choice of method that suits the practitioner. This is a very 'user friendly' approach permitting the construction of a custom-built practice best suited to the needs and difficulties of individual trainees. Furthermore, he is extremely cautious about encouraging his trainees to seek Enlightenment in a way that presupposes craving and creates a misleading tension and expectations. Words like Enlightenment and kensho rarely pass his lips. He makes it quite clear that his retreats are for the development of practice. Like Dogen, the great Japanese Soto master and philosopher, I suspect he sees training and enlightenment as inseparable. To Shih-fu the purpose of retreat is as follows:

1. To realise one is not in control of one's own mind.
2. To discover how to train one's mind in awareness.
3. To calm the mind.
4. To provide opportunities for repentence and hence to regain immaculacy.
5. To practise with an individually suitable method that will yield insight (*prajna*).

The methods used are: Watching the breath, Counting the breath, Hua-t'ou practice and Serene Illumination. As will be discussed in the talks that follow, the purpose of watching and counting the breath is to lock the mind onto an intentional act so that wandering thoughts are reduced. With practice it becomes possible to shift the attention from the breath itself to the mental 'space' within which the breathing happens.

The hua-t'ou is a short phrase, often in the form of a question, which may be a crucial point or punch line from a koan story. While an attempt to analyse the question 'Who is dragging this old corpse along?' may help to exhaust the mind of intellection and hence lead to a non-conceptual insight,[4] a more direct approach is simply to witness the space in which this question moves. This process is sometimes described by the Chinese word *ts'an* which means to enter, to go into or to penetrate. In the current context, this means seeing the whole of a process rather than a part. In Hsu-yun's teaching, it is the task of the trainee to shift his attention from being a 'guest' to being a 'host'. The guest is a wandering thought, a breath or a hua-t'ou. The guest stands like a figure against a background which is the host. The practitioner's attention is gradually moved away from the figure into the ground.

Although Master Sheng Yen may use the contemplation of a koan as a method, he is wary of it. The habit of working with antique stories is like resurrecting dead corpses, he says. Unless a trainee can bring them to life, old koans are dead koans. Furthermore, familiarity with them shows that many are essentially similar so that it becomes possible to 'crack' a series of related koans quickly. This calls into question a system in which advancement through a series of koans constitutes progress. Cracking one may crack a set, but is this one resolution or many? The only relevant koans, says Shih-fu, are those that refer to the self in its present situation. The only live koan is actually yourself. As Dogen said, the koan arises in daily life. It is not essential to fabricate one. When the Chinese monk Daikaku came to Kamakura in the thirteenth century, he knew little Japanese and his students knew little of the Chinese classical Ch'an literature. So, instead of classical koans, he invented simple direct questions arising out of the immediate experiences of his trainees, the so called Kamakura warrior koans.[5] The method was vibrant and yielded a positive response. This is instructive for westerners today.

Methods such as watching the breath or ts'an with a hua-t'ou are to be done within the maintenance of a firm sitting posture facing a wall. Shih-fu emphasises the desirability of an alert formal posture, back erect but not strained, head straight with slight forward inclination, crossed legs and eyes open. However, he is not as insistent on the maintenance of an unmoving posture as are some Japanese teachers. He recognises that most lay Westerners, who do not spend many hours per week meditating, have difficulties with maintaining the appropriate posture over the long hours of a retreat. There is a lot of leg and back pain. For these relatively amateur practitioners, it is more significant to develop the mental practice than to agonise over the body too intensively. The use of stools and variant postures are therefore tolerated and movements may be made so long as they are restrained.

Shikantaza or 'just sitting' is the prime method of the Soto tradition in Japan. In the Ts'ao-tung of China the parallel method is Serene Illumination (*Mo-chao*). In this practice, the maintenance of a firm posture is important and the mind meditates upon its own stillness. The difficulties in remaining within this stillness are considerable, primarily because of the rising of wandering thoughts and drowsiness. Unlike working with a hua-t'ou, the mind has not been given an intentional task and it is all the more difficult to set wandering thought aside, Shih-fu says[6] that he does not often recommend this method, in spite of its frequent use in Zen circles. This is because to benefit from it there needs to be a firm practice already established. If the mind is much given to wandering, the attempt to practise Serene Illumination can be frustrating and non-productive. 'You must be at a stage where there's no problem becoming settled, when you can sit with unbroken concentration, with almost no outside thoughts . . . [Otherwise] It is hard to tell whether your mind is "bright and open" or just blank. You can be idling, having very subtle thoughts, and believe you are practising Silent Illumination. You can be silent without illuminating anything.' There needs to be both serenity and illumination present in a mutual reinforcement. Yet the method once acquired is very powerful:

> Silently and serenely one forgets all words,
> Clearly and vividly IT appears before you.
> When one realises IT, time has no limits
> When experienced, your surroundings come to life.[7]

In a conversation with me, Shih-fu compared the methods of koan and Serene Illumination. In koan practice the mind generates a great 'mass of doubt' as it seeks to penetrate the meaning of the example. Similarly the hua-t'ou may generate the same doubt. The intensity of this inquiry is such that the mind is literally possessed by preoccupation with the koan. There is no room for anything else. In the course of the work all aspects of personal being are drawn into this central inferno of questioning. Bodily aches and pains, personal karma, unresolved relationships, metaphysical anxieties, alienation from the divine, the thought of death, all are dragged together to one point. When the mind is fully unified the whole person has gathered at one 'place'. It is at this place that resolution may suddenly occur. Shih-fu's own first experience of kensho was of this type (see p 115).

'Seeing the nature' does not always arise precisely in this manner. Sometimes it appears, as it were, capriciously, following long periods of profound focus. Master Hsu-yun, after a period of deep concentration, was taking tea. Suddenly, as tea was being poured, he dropped the cup. Then it happened. The nun Shiyono, after years of unenlightened endeavour, was crossing the yard at night carrying a pail of water. The moon shone and was reflected in the bucket. Suddenly the bamboo handle broke and the water spilled all over the yard. 'No more water, no more moon – emptiness in my hand.'[8]

Shih-fu acknowledges that transcendental or mystical experiences, perhaps of a psychologically identical form, occur naturally in many religious practices and also to poets, (such as Wordsworth), naturalists (such as Thoreau or Richard Jefferies), indeed to almost anyone. The significance of the kensho in Ch'an, said Shih-fu, is related to a firm understanding of the Dharma. An understanding that the self is not an inherently existing object but rather the expression of co-determining mental causes and conditions (*pratitya samutpada*) provides the kensho experience with its unique insight into the flow of impermanence.

The practice of Silent Illumination yields insight in a rather different way. Here there is a gradual stilling of the mind into a thoughtless state. A similar condition is reached by the methods of *ts'an* focussing on breath or hua-t'ou. The mind, that endless social calculus, comes to an end and an illumination of quiet joy arises, a release into a pure awareness reflecting that-which-is as if in a mirror. It is from such a point that 'seeing the nature' happens. In D. T. Suzuki's phrase this consists in 'the absence of the separateness implied by being conscious of' either oneself or of the koan.[9] In the absence of this split between subject and object there is simply what-is, shining with a pristine clarity.

In retreat with Shih-fu, the use of one of these methods is negotiated in interview. Shih-fu takes into account the understanding of self and life shown by the practitioner's presence at interview and also his or her prior work within the Dharma. However, a rigidity of method is not imposed. Shih-fu's emphasis is very much on flexibility according to what arises. For example, a koan may suddenly arise within the context of watching the breath. According to context, Shih-fu may suggest that such a koan should then be followed. This parallels Dogen's view that koans arise in everyday life and do not have to be preconstituted. Although Shih-fu's English remains limited and he gives talks with an interpreter, he interviews directly in this language. He is not so much concerned with what is being said but with what is happening within the individual process. Westerners testify to his acute perception which transcends the barriers of language.

The task of the master on retreat is to facilitate the movement of the practitioner towards a deeper and more insightful practice. Sometimes this may involve draconian methods, as when a fierce approach can deepen the mass of doubt to breaking point. Such fierceness may be entirely appropriate in the Rinzai tradition. It is a paradoxical aspect of compassion. Yet, where trainees with a range of aptitudes and methods are present, a more balanced approach is required and quick responsiveness to a range of trainee conditions. I have been told that when Shih-fu first gave retreats in New York he was much fiercer, using the kyosaku (the master's 'incense' stick) liberally to assist sitters, and flipping it lightly at legs to speed up fast running in the gaps between sessions. Today, his approach is milder reflecting the aptitudes of his sitters, all of whom are lay people from a wide range of walks of life.

The personal interview (*dokusan*) is the key element in the contact between master and trainee. Shih-fu has the ability to assume many appearances. At interview he may appear remote, severe, totally detached and disinterested, even withering, waiting for you to produce something worthwhile and dismissing you when you don't. Or he may appear compassionate and caring while always returning the problem to the trainee. He may be humorous, engaging one as he would a close friend. He may reveal an unfathomable depth that leaves the mind groping to go after him. There may be silence or speech. There is always presence. Each participant comes to know him through his own karma. Shih-fu is a master of skilful means.

RITUAL IN RETREAT

Chanting and repetition of dharanis or mantras form part of the liturgies which punctuate the retreat every morning and evening. These liturgies, chanted or spoken in both Chinese and English, are shortened versions of the daily monastic practices. Liturgical practice locates the retreat within the lineage and brings up feelings of aspiration and gratitude. The Heart Sutra is a central pivot of the liturgy in both the morning and evening services evoking the centrality of the insight into Form as Emptiness and Emptiness as Form. Here the pivotal position of the philosophical view stemming from the Prajnaparamita sutras is reaffirmed.

Every morning we chant Samantabhadra Bodhisattva's Ten Vows:

The first, to worship and respect all Buddhas.
The second, to praise the Tathagatas.
The third, to cultivate the giving of offerings.
The fourth, to repent all karmic obstructions.
The fifth, to rejoice in the merits of others.
The sixth, to request the turning of the Dharma wheel.
The seventh, to request that the Buddhas dwell in the World.

The eighth, to always follow the Buddhas in study.
The ninth, to always harmonise with living beings.
The tenth, to transfer all merits to others.

This is followed by the Four Great Vows;

I vow to deliver innumerable sentient beings.
I vow to cut off endless vexations.
I vow to master limitless approaches to Dharma.
I vow to attain Supreme Buddhahood.

The morning liturgy ends with the Three Refuges:

I take refuge in Buddha and I wish all sentient beings
will awaken to the Great Path and make the Supreme
Resolution.
I take refuge in Dharma and I wish all sentient beings
will penetrate the Sutras, their wisdom as deep as the
ocean.
I take refuge in Sangha, and I wish all sentient beings
will be brought together in Great Harmony without any
obstructions at all.

The evening liturgy is the Meng-shan Liturgy of Food
Bestowal. This is an offering of spiritual food to all sentient
beings, and especially to the Lonely Souls and Hungry
Ghosts wandering between lives in karmic distress. One may
interpret this literally, as was no doubt the original intention,
or read into it the meaning that all of us at some time or
another are ourselves Lonely Souls or Hungry Ghosts beset
with grasping and desire and experiencing the depths of
depression or other hells of the mind. The liturgy begins
with the important statement:

To know all the Buddhas
of the past, present and future
perceive that Dharmadhatu nature
is all created by the mind.[10]

There follows a series of mantras or power words the recitations of which have the following functions: firstly to break the powers of Hell, secondly to invite all beings universally to the Offering, thirdly to loosen their knots of oppression. Homages and the Three Refuges are then chanted. A general repentence is then made:

All bad karma created by Buddhists, Sentient Beings and Lonely Souls, comes from greed, hatred and ignorance since time without beginning arising out of body, speech and mind. For all this the beings do repent.

Mantras then continue; to absolve karmic obstructions, to open the constricted throats of Hungry Ghosts, to affirm the precepts, to convert the food into Amrita. More homages to the Tathagatas follow and then the food is blessed:

Powerful Mantras bless the pure food given universally to beings as countless as the Ganges' sands. May they all give up grudging and greed and quickly escape darkness to be born in the Pure land (etc).

The food (rice and water mixed at the time) is then offered with the wish that the merits of the offering be extended everywhere. Mantras of offering are recited as the food is taken outside and donated. The Heart Sutra follows and the Four Great Vows. The assembly is then warned:

This day has passed.
Our lives too are closing,
Like fish with little water
Joy will not last.
Let us work with pure effort,
Work as we would were our heads aflame.
Be mindful of impermanence.
Be careful of idleness.

The ceremony closes with the Three Refuges and a short prayer transferring merit to others.[11]

THIS BOOK AND ITS TEXT

Shih-fu's talks were spoken in Mandarin Chinese and are available on tapes. His words were translated immediately by Ming Yee Wang and these English renderings have been used to construct the text of this book. My task as editor was not an easy one. I took Ming Yee's words and turned them back into what I considered would have been their form in the first person as spoken by Shih-fu. For example, most of the interpretations began with the phrase 'Shih-fu says . . .'. This had to be rendered as if he was himself speaking in the first person. An alternative procedure of course would have been to get a further written translation of the Chinese tapes made. This would have been prohibitively expensive and not necessarily more revealing of Shih-fu's intentions. In any case, extensive editing to remove inessential material, specific comment on the moment and repetition was essential. In effect, I was engaging in an exercise in hermeneutics, an interpretation of Shih-fu's teaching in which my own subjectivity was highly engaged.[12] There are some sections of the text where, the tape not being explicit, I allowed my intuition to lead me in the choice of words or phrasing. I can only hope that this approach has not led to any serious misunderstanding of the Dharma. Shih-fu, in consultation with Ming Yee Wang, has approved this text.

The talks are presented in the order in which they were given. The reader should know however that these talks were of two kinds. Talks given in the early morning and at meal times were immediate responses to the retreat situations and offered specific comment or instructions to the participants. The evening talks were discourses upon the poem *Calming the Mind* by Wang Ming, a Chinese master of the sixth century CE. Shih-fu has said that his presentation of this poem was geared to the instruction of practitioners many of whom were beginners. He has not addressed his theme from the point of view of scholarship as he would have done if he were addressing an academic audience. Essentially we have here Shih-fu's own meditations on *Calming the Mind* as a transmission of the Wisdom of the Patriarchs in our time. The reader may wish to examine these talks in their natural sequence or to select the evening talks as a separate series. In either case, let us now proceed to listen. As Shih-fu said, this is an auspicious opportunity.

For the convenience of readers, the text of *Calming the Mind* is now provided in a complete form as translated by Shih-fu and his collaborators:[13]

Too much knowledge leads to overactivity;
Better to calm the mind.
The more you consider, the greater the loss;
Better to unify the mind.

Excessive thinking weakens the will.
The more you know, the more your mind is confused.
A confused mind gives rise to vexation.
The weakened will obstructs the Tao.

Don't say there is no harm in this;
The ensuing pain may last forever.
Don't think there is nothing to fear;
The calamities churn like bubbles in a boiling pot.

Water dripping ceaselessly
Will fill the four seas.
Specks of dust not wiped away
Will become the five mountains*.

Protect the branches to save the roots;
Though a small matter, it is not trivial.
Close the seven orifices†,
Shut off the six senses‡.

Pay no heed to forms;
Do not listen to sounds.
Listening to sounds you become deaf,
You become blind observing forms.

Literature and art
Are but busy gnats in the air;
Technique and ability
A solitary lamp in the sun.

Those able and talented ones
Are really stupid fellows.
Discarding the pure and simple
They drown in too much beauty.

Consciousness is an untamed horse,
The mind an unruly monkey.
If the spirit is overactive,
The body will sicken and die.

Wrong conduct ends in delusion;
Those treading this path become mired in mud.
To regard ability as precious
Is called confusion.

To exaggerate clumsiness and covet skill
Does not lead to great virtue.
Of much fame but little contribution,
Their reputation quickly crumbles.

Merely reading books
Is of no lasting value.
Being inwardly proud
Brings the enmity of others.

Using speech
Or written words
To gain the praise of others
Is something most repulsive.

What common people regard as auspicious
The sage takes as evil.
The enjoyment gained is fleeting,
But the sorrow is everlasting.

Beware of shadows and tracks;
The farther you leave them, the better.
Sitting upright in the shade of a tree,
Neither traces nor shadows remain.

Worries of birth and distress of old age
Are products of your own thoughts.
If the mind's thinking is ended,
Birth and death are forever cut off.

Not dying, not born,
Without form or name,
The Tao is empty and tranquil.
The myriad phenomena are equal.

What is of value? What is cheap?
Where is there shame or glory?
What is excellent or inferior?
How can there be heavy and light?

The clear sky puts purity to shame.
No brightness compares with the brilliant sun.
Stable as Mount T'ai;
Steady as a golden wall.

I respectfully present this poem to all virtuous ones
So that this Tao will forever remain.

* The five mountains in China having a sacred connection with the Buddha (analogous to the five sacred mountains of India): Ching Shan, Pei Shan, Nan Shan, King Asoka Shan, T'ai Po Shan.
† The seven orifices: two eyes, two ears, two nostrils, and mouth.
‡ The six senses: sight, hearing, smell, taste, touch and mental perception.

NOTES

1. See accounts of the history of Buddhism in China, for example K. Ch'en, 1964, *Buddhism in China*, (Princeton University Press, Princeton). Also articles in J. M. Kitagawa and M. D.

Cummings, 1989, *Buddhism in Asian History*. Selections from the
Encyclopedia of Religion (ed. M. Eliade) (Macmillan, London).
2. See the valuable discussion of mahayana philosophy in P.
Williams, 1989, *Mahayana Buddhism: the doctrinal foundations*,
(Routledge, London).
3. See R. Fields, 1981, *How the Swans came to the Lake*, (Shambala,
Boston), p. 234.
4. For an excellent discussion of the usage of these methods and
the terms describing them the reader should consult the article
by Master Sheng Yen entitled 'Tso-Ch'an' in the *Chung-Hwa
Buddhist Journal*, Vol 2, pp. 361–386, 1988. For Hsu-yun's
approach, see Lu Kuan Yu, 1960, *Ch'an and Zen Teaching. First
series*, (Century, London). The use of the Hua-t'ou in the
Communication Exercise of Charles Berner's 'Enlightenment
Intensive' as used in Western Zen retreats is discussed in
Crook's two chapters in J. H. Crook and D. Fontana, (eds),
1990, *Space in Mind: East–West Psychology and Contemporary
Buddhism*, (Element Books, Shaftesbury).
5. See T. Leggett, 1985, *The Warrior Koans: Early Zen in Japan*,
(Arkana, Harmondsworth).
6. See Sheng Yen, 1982, *Getting the Buddha Mind* (Dharma Drum,
New York, p. 78 *et seq*. Also see his chapter on Zen meditation
in K. Kraft (ed.), 1988, *Zen Tradition and Transition: An
Overview of Zen in the Modern World*, (Rider, London).
7. From 'Silent Illumination', by Hung-chih Cheng-chueh,
(1091–1157). See *Getting the Buddha Mind* (Dharma Drum,
New York) p. 75. Note: I have provided capitalisations to
make an emphasis.
8. See Bhagwan Shree Rajneesh, 1975, *No Water, No Moon*
(*Rajneesh* Foundation, India).
9. See R. Fields, 1981, *How the Swans Came to the Lake* (Shambhala,
Boston), p. 138.
10. The meaning here is that all Buddhas have realised that
everything that is experienced is a mental representation. As
such it is capable of change through our own actions. We are
responsible for our own experiencing. We are not victims of
outside forces.
11. Wording edited from the Liturgy for Morning and Evening
Services. Ch'an Meditation Center, 90–56 Corona Avenue,
Elmhurst, New York 11373. The mantras themselves are the
Chinese pronunciations of originally Sanskrit mantras of great
antiquity. Dr D. T. Suzuki has attempted to provide the
Sanskrit originals and their English equivalents. See his *Manual*

of Zen Buddhism, 1950 (Rider, London), second impression 1956, pp. 17–18.

12. Habermas understands a hermeneutic exercise of this kind as one in which 'the meaning discloses itself to the interpreter only to the extent that his own world becomes clarified at the same time. The subject of understanding establishes communication between both worlds.' See *Knowledge and Human Interests*, 1971, (Beacon Press, Boston). Original publication 1968, p. 309. See also the discussion of hermeneutic work in East–West psychology by Anand Peranjpe in his Introduction to A. C. Peranjpe, D. Y. F. Ho and R. W. Reiber, 1988, *Asian Contributions to Psychology*, (Praeger, New York), pp. 31–32.

13. See Sheng Yen, Master, 1987, *The Poetry of Enlightenment. Poems by Ancient Chinese Masters* (Dharma Drum, New York).

1 THE DHARMA DISCOURSES OF MASTER SHENG YEN

I EXPECT some of you can understand that getting to Wales has been somewhat like undergoing a Ch'an retreat! For the last three days we have spent over fifty hours on planes without a proper night's sleep and with a complete uncertainty as to whether we were actually going to arrive! Yet, here we are. And I can see you are all ready to begin. Everything is arranged. You all have your places marked and your jobs allocated. So we must certainly start at once.

You know that I intended to come here last year, but at that time we were not aware that I had to have a visa. Then, this year, we got the visa but, when we arrived at the Taipei airport, we found it had just expired. What an obstruction! The only thing to do was to fly at once to New York where it would be easy to get another visa. So we spent a few hours in New York and got on another plane. Would you believe it – the plane developed a fault before take off and we all had to disembark. Of course we were very tired even by that time. You can understand that at the moment the only thought in my head is sleep. I shall not say very much now.

Actually I should tell you that we almost gave up the idea of coming. But then I thought of all the work you have done – John especially – in arranging this event, and I felt that on no account could I let you down. So here I am. This is then a very precious occasion. Despite numerous obstacles it has come about. I hope each one of you will treasure the opportunity and work hard.

Now you tell me: How many of you have never experienced a retreat before? How many of you have done three or more retreats? Has anybody participated specifically in a retreat in the Soto tradition? Or in the Rinzai tradition? Has anybody read one of my books? Oh – two of them! Great. You will know that Zen, Ch'an in Chinese, is not for the purpose of getting instant Enlightenment? Rather the practice itself is the goal. Most people think that 'seeing into one's own nature' using some method of instant Enlightenment is a convenient and speedy path. But this is a severely erroneous understanding. Of course there is 'Enlightenment'. But mostly there are false enlightenments. If you are very anxious to get enlightened, you can precipitate a kind of mistaken experience which you call enlightenment. That can be very sad.

After so much difficulty in getting here, I have not come to give you Enlightenment. That is absurd. Rather I have come to see whether it is possible to pass on to you the methods whereby you can improve your practice. It is like eating. We cannot expect to be filled by taking one mouthful and munching once or twice. We need to digest a whole meal until we know we have had enough. We are going to use the methods of practice to benefit the body and mind. That is the most important thing.

There are a number of methods one can use. In the first interviews I will discuss with each one of you which method is best suited to your needs. To begin with, if you are in doubt, just count the breath. The other methods are 'Silent Illumination', which is similar to 'Searching the Heart' of the Japanese Soto School. There are also the hua-t'ou and koan methods. We shall talk about these.

Just as we had problems getting to Wales, so too will you encounter obstructions in the practice of your method. These arise from your own mind and body, not from elsewhere. One simply has to persist and continue with practice. Be prepared for struggle. We have six days ahead of us and even to recognise the obstructions is, in itself, the beginning of true practice.

In this small house we are hidden away in the mountains. The moment is auspicious. Now – sit.

DAY ONE – THE FIRST TALK

First of all, we must understand that in Ch'an there is no fixed method. Each retreat is unique. It adapts itself to whoever is present, to the environment and to the time. I am responsive to these things and trust intuitively in the way I feel things can develop. Perhaps it is like going to a restaurant and looking at the menu. Except that, at the moment, the menu is blank. Since this is my first visit to your country, we will work out together the best way to proceed. Maybe the style of New York or Taiwan is not suited to a small farmhouse in the hills of Wales. We shall see.

To begin let us set out some basic rules for the retreat.

No talking. Of course, for some jobs a few words need to be spoken; especially in arranging the cooking for example. But, apart from such necessary interactions, there should be no conversation whatsoever. Talking about how you are, or how you think the retreat is going, is of no help to practice. It is just an interference and it wastes the energy of a focussed mind.

No noise. Keep yourselves tidy and quiet.

No thinking! For some tasks you need to consider what you are doing or to plan the sequence of your actions. But for many jobs thinking is not essential. Just let the hands do it. Let the mind be on whatever you are doing. Just do it, don't evaluate it or compare yourself with others. Put your mind on the job, on the eating, on the toilet. You do not need to judge what you are eating. All you need to do is fill the stomach to have the energy to practise.

No looking at others. It is of no value to you to see how others are doing or coping with problems. On a retreat to consider how others are, is to fill the mind with inessential concerns. It is not your business.

No looking about, no listening to pleasing sounds. Keep the senses quiet. If you look around at the scenery you will start judging it. 'How beautiful the sunshine! Oh dear; here comes the rain!' Likewise with sounds, bird songs, tractors, sheep baaing. Treat them all the same. Pay no attention. Of course you will see and hear. But do not intentionally look about or listen evaluatively. The aim is to stop the sources of discrimination.

No analysis of whatever is said in the talks or instructions. If I say something that is helpful to you, fine! If not – forget it!

Maintain your separateness. Each of you is quite independent. Don't pay any attention to whoever is sitting next to you, whether they are complaining or happy. In this world, all you know is yourself – nobody else. And, in fact, you don't know yourself either. The best thing on retreat is to keep the mind a blank – filled only with practice.

Be on time. There are plenty of toilets so there is no need to be late when the bell rings or the boards are struck. Indeed, unless you are sick or there is some special reason, you should always be early and ready to sit on time.

The whole day is practice. Whether we are sitting, doing exercises, slow or fast walking, prostrations or cooking, listening to a talk – the whole focus is on the practice.

Now some questions for you.

How old is the youngest here? And the oldest?

Has anybody a heart problem, high blood pressure, migraines or other ailments?

Is anybody undergoing psychotherapy?

Who has had beneficial experiences from meditation of any kind previously?

We have all discovered the schedule and been taught the signals for the various events. We will talk about posture and methods individually. I shall only use the stick if you wish for it. It may be valuable when you are sleepy or distracted. But you must ask me. I won't use it unless you ask.

Now we can start. As many of you already know something

of the benefits of meditation, we can have a valuable training period. Let us have six memorable days together. Interviews will begin this afternoon.

DAY ONE – EVENING TALK

I have only been in your country for a day but already I have learnt something about you people. You have a love for ancient things. This house is hundreds of years old. You treasure the old worm-eaten beams and the crumbling stone walls, the bent timbers of the old barn. In Taiwan we are busily engaged in pulling everything down and building up the new. In Ch'an, we treasure the old while making it always new. So it is appropriate here that I should talk to you about one of the oldest of the Chinese scriptures.

I don't know what was happening in Britain in the sixth century. In China it was the time of the Liang Dynasty (502–556 CE). Buddhism was already established and Ch'an was developing. Yet, in those early years, the Chinese did not distinguish too clearly between their own Taoist ideas and those of the new religion. So in this text you will find a number of Taoist ideas which give a particular flavour to the Ch'an of that period.

The text is so ancient that we are not sure who wrote it. He is known as Wang Ming, but that may be a pseudonym. His surname was Sung and he served as a government official; but when the dynasty ended, he became a monk and took his vows under a Ch'an master. His intellectual ability implies that he studied theory with numerous teachers.

Wang Ming emphasises the unification of mind as especially important and this goes back both to old Taoist notions and to the Indian idea of bringing the mind to single-pointedness. He calls his poem 'Calming the Mind' and it is a valuable one for beginners. It describes the method of practice and how to do it. Wang Ming advises us to let go of our anxieties and vexations and to let life unroll naturally.

In the poem, 'Mind' can be used in two senses. As we shall

see, the first usage refers to the worried mind of discrimination, the tense mind that needs to relax. It is this mind to which the title refers. Yet when the mind becomes relaxed what is the 'Mind' then? This is the second usage – a mind beyond illusion, discrimination and the need to relax.

One of you has remarked how difficult it is to concentrate. Which mind are you trying to concentrate? We must be certain that we speak here of the mind of illusion that needs to become calm in order to see clearly. It is the mind that discriminates and then favours one thing more than another that always creates tensions.

When you try to calm the mind, there are two important principles. We need to be clear about these. The first is to cease worrying and the second is not to be concerned with knowledge. For your practice to be effective, you don't have to worry and you don't need to understand intellectually.

We would like to be able to concentrate fully on our method, be it counting the breath, silent awareness or working with a koan. Yet the more we try, the less concentration we achieve. Our minds simply do not obey our intentions. We try to stay with the method but, before we know where we are, the mind has drifted away onto something else. Our attitude is wrong somewhere; we feel frustrated and lost.

This morning I asked you to leave behind, for the moment, all those people and events with whom you have been relating. We should stop thinking about the ongoing problems of our lives and relationships. Of course these things are important and after the retreat we shall take up such issues again. But here and now, in the retreat, we should let them go. Keep your distance from the past and the future. What is it that makes this so difficult?

Mostly the thoughts that arise are concerned with the past – or perhaps with the future that will arise as a result of the past. This involves discrimination, judgement, comparison and memory; it provokes an anxious tension that varies in strength according to the topic that comes up and your own disposition. It is vital to practise putting all this down. Just put it down. Leave aside all past, all knowledge. With practice you can let it go. When you can do this for as long as you wish, you have found a certain freedom.

Please do not misunderstand me. It is not that knowledge and experience are to be avoided or condemned. Rather knowledge and experience are to be valued, but we need to gain control of their use. If we leave them to ramble haphazardly through our heads sowing worries and agitation then they become a burden to us, a vexation and an obstacle. Some people spend all night worrying; others put away their thoughts and sleep soundly. We need to cultivate the art of putting aside our memories, our concerns and our intellectual knowledge.

The first verse of the poem reads:

> Too much knowledge leads to overactivity;
> Better to calm the mind.
> The more you consider, the greater the loss;
> Better to unify the mind.

The more you know, the more things can cause you distress. When you know little you can be simple. In practising, do not consider what you are doing intellectually or theoretically. All you need to do is the practice. Use it to replace everything else.

When you are confused and filled with conceptual fog you may get depressed and struggle. It is important not to become too judgemental. In fact, any thought is illusory; it is never the thing in itself. Whatever you think is illusory. Illusion is normal! Do not be afraid of the rambling mind nor condemn it angrily. The important thing is simply to recognise the state of thought that at that moment inhabits you. Recognising an illusory thought will usually get rid of it. To have an aversion to thought is to sustain yet another level of illusion.

In Chinese, the sentence 'Better to unify the mind' can be translated as 'Guard the one'. What is this one? There are two meanings here. The first applies to the mind that is split up, discriminating, filled with illusory intellection. This mind needs to be focussed, brought to a single point. Guarding the one means bringing the mind to this single place. And that is done through the method of practice.

Training is portrayed in the Ch'an tradition by the parable of the ox herder. The ox has to be trained to do its job and not wander about over other people's gardens. To begin with, the ox herder must use his whip and apply discipline. Later the ox is tamed; when eating it eats, when drawing the plough, it pulls. It does the thing in hand undistractedly. This is guarding the one.

Once the mind has come to a single point, the term acquires a further meaning. The mind is now no longer practising. It has arrived. The whip can be put away. Three things are happening: (i) Body and mind are one. (ii) Internal and External are unified. (iii) Previous thought and subsequent thought are continuous.

No longer is there an experience of the mind separate from the body, regarding the body as something different. No longer is the observer separate from the observed; and experience flows without time being split into now and then. These three conditions arise together; if one is present, so are the others. Once the mind is unified, so the one is guarded.

I am sure those of you who have participated in several retreats have had some experience of this. Is it not so?

> Excessive thinking weakens the will.
> The more you know, the more your mind is confused.
> A confused mind gives rise to vexation.
> The weakened will obstructs the Tao.

Again do not fall into the mistaken belief that Ch'an is anti-intellectual. I myself have persevered in scholarly studies and looked into theories and explanations and so have many of you. These lines refer to the inappropriateness of thinking in the context of practice. Sometimes somebody comes to me with an answer to a koan. I may ask where he got it from. Sometimes it obviously comes from a book. The answer has been a consequence of knowledge, of thinking. It is not an answer arising from a mind free of illusion. This is not wisdom. If you are relying on books or theories or other people's descriptions, you can never solve a koan. The wisdom of the book is not the wisdom of seeing. If you deliberate, you are far from the mark. If you are far from the mark, you are confused and there will be vexation. If there is intellectual doubt, there is only faulty awakening.

DAY TWO – EARLY MORNING
(4.15 am)

I have three words for the day. These words are:

Isolation
Non-Dependence and
Non-Attachment.

The purpose of these words is to give you a focus for attention within your practice, an awareness from moment to moment whether in sitting or in relation to the group while you are working or eating.

Isolation means keeping your self separate from the environment and from others. Isolation is an attitude of practice. Even though you are sitting and working with others, let it be as if you were the only one here, as if there was only one sitting place in the meditation hall, in the whole building. It is as if you are alone, a solitary practitioner in the mountains. It is important sometimes to withdraw and to be solitary, to be isolated and separate. Usually we are in constant interaction with the environment – our everyday worlds. We are disturbed by the ongoing concerns of the world, the news bulletins, the politics of the capital, new taxes, old commitments. All this involvement causes us to lose touch with our basic being. We get filled with the noise of the world. If you isolate yourself in practice, from past and from future, just being present, then you can see your self-nature more easily, without interferences. As you go into this you may eventually isolate yourself from previous thought, and again from subsequent thought. As you withdraw from your own thoughts, you begin to discover what the independent self – the unconditioned – is.

By *Non-Dependence* I mean not being concerned with what others are thinking, doing or saying. Most of our lives are spent in some sort of adjustment to other people who we want to influence in some way. Maybe we want to please somebody, or we feel obliged in some way; or we owe somebody a favour; or we may want to reject or harm somebody. We are driven by our involvement with others and cannot let it go. This is dependency. When we let ourselves be ourselves, we are not involved with others. We may still be concerned about other people but not dependent on their thoughts, attitudes or opinions.

Even here on a retreat – with the rules of silence and such – where it would seem easy to be free of dependency, you may not find it so. You may be aware of others' attitudes; you may develop feelings of attraction or repulsion towards an other; you may be concerned whether I am thinking well or unfavourably about you. You are not independent in your inner self. You are still bound by habits of dependence which you are throwing out around you as you sit or as you work. If this is the case, notice it. Separate yourself. Find a mind that is not dependent on others. Even if you are afraid of loneliness, you need to experiment with this to make progress.

You need to train yourself so that at any time and any moment you choose, you can free yourself inwardly from your world, from others, from the past, from the future, from the previous thought and the next thought. That is to find freedom. Yet if you then think you are free and have some wisdom, this is not so. You should not be attached to solitude or to experiences of relative freedom. When you are neither attached to independence nor to company then wisdom will manifest.

Isolation and independence constitute *Non-Attachment*. I mean non-attachment to your self, to the devices by which you make yourself safe. When you go beyond this illusory safety, you find freedom and wisdom; and from wisdom, as you look at the world, comes compassion.

DAY TWO – LUNCH TIME REMARKS

Whether we can get to that stage where the mind and body are united within practice depends on whether we can relax our tensions and allow the body to be at ease.

Maybe this is like somebody trying to ride a horse. For a beginner the motion of the horse is very tiring. Even for an accomplished equestrian, if the horse is a wild one the rider can have an exhausting time. Yet, for a beginner with a tamed horse or a skilled rider with a wild one, the riding can become comfortable and effortless. The rider and the steed are one. There is no feeling of struggle or separation.

If the body is having a hard time – getting tired of sitting for example – then we feel fatigued from effort. Yet, when the method runs along smoothly, we forget about the body and mind because they are united. We feel pleasant and relaxed.

When we meditate for long periods, it is important to forget the body. Likewise in retreat, when we have a task to do, just do it and do not be concerned with how the mind feels.

If the mind is scattered when we are doing a task, then many thoughts arise, one after the other. The mind separates from the action of the body. If we concentrate on the task, just performing it, cutting up the carrots, for example, or cleaning the table, or sweeping the floor, then we are unaware of the mind.

This is the second day of the retreat. On the first day most people are not accustomed to the system of the retreat. Now that it is the second day, whether you are meditating or doing your task, let your mind and your bodily actions be one. Do not allow them to become separate.

Don't say there is no harm in this;
the ensuing pain may last forever.
Don't think there is nothing to fear;
the calamities churn like bubbles in a
boiling pot.

Wang Ming does not intend us to take him lightly. He is very
much in earnest. He says that if we cannot put down the
habit of reasoning, of turning our knowledge over and over,
then we cannot obtain the benefits of meditation. To continue
with such a habit constitutes a serious problem. No one should
think there is nothing to fear. Rather, you need to know that
such a habit generates harm that can continue indefinitely.

In the sutras there is a particular term which points at our
capacity for tolerating this world of suffering. Although we
recognise that this is a world of suffering, we continue to put
up with it. Not only that; we are willingly tolerant of suffering. We remain attached to the concerns of worldly life, the
worries, the vanities and the discriminatory categories we use
to judge one another. This is a world where we endlessly
cope with suffering and rarely go beyond it.

Likewise, a practitioner of Ch'an may know very well that
wandering discursive thoughts are potentially harmful, but
none the less he may remain positively attracted to them.
After all they are amusing. When told not to entertain such
tantalising ideas and to think of nothing, the practitioner
soon finds practice very boring. For example, we have
agreed not to talk to one another. We know very well that
talking causes us to lose our meditative focus. None the less
situations arise in which a few remarks are passed. We cannot
resist prolonging the interaction with a few more words in
reply. It seems such an enjoyable thing.

Since we are indeed serious about practice, we should not
think lightly of these warnings. If we heed them, we can go
beyond knowledge and true practice can begin.

Water dripping ceaselessly
will fill the four seas.
Specks of dust not wiped away
will become the five mountains.

Don't think that a tiny bit of wandering thought is irrelevant. Maybe there is only a tiny bit of wandering thought in this sitting, this day, this retreat. But the accumulation of these tiny wandering thoughts becomes one gigantic wandering thought – a monster.

This habit has been formed since time without beginning. Endlessly we are judging things and one another by using our knowledge and our memory of past experiences; and this has been passed down from life to life. Indeed it is karma itself. We are this habit, entangled and constrained within it; and of this we are unaware.

When we focus in practice, it becomes quite easy to see the truth of this. We can see the scattered thoughts and the perseveration, the endless cycling of our limited and caging ideas and judgements, our prejudices. And the clearer we see such things the better the chance of our success.

Now, in the last two days what have you found to be the most difficult element in practice? Is it when we are dozing off or is it when we have wandering thoughts? Those troubled by dozing off please raise your hands. And those with wandering thoughts.

When sleepiness is the greater problem, it may be due to lack of energy or to a temporary malaise, a cold or a virus. If you are practising well and a great sleepiness comes then sometimes there is nothing that can really help. If you become very exhausted then it is important to take a rest. But if you lack energy through laziness or are merely a little drowsy, then if you increase your breathing, take some fresh air or do some exercises you may energise yourself again.

In fact, Wang Ming doesn't discuss the problem of falling asleep. Perhaps in his day practitioners never lacked energy! The remaining problem is the wandering thoughts.

Do you know how to deal with wandering thoughts? The first step is to recognise when the mind is wandering. Often it comes over you so subtly that you do not even notice it. Then suddenly we say; Oh, what on Earth am I thinking about? So we have to be mindful of what we are doing in our practice. And when we do detect that our minds have wandered, it is important not to feel irritated with oneself or an aversion towards the thoughts. It simply tires you out if you take up a belligerent attitude towards your own mind! The paradoxical thing is that very often, as soon as you recognise the fact of wandering, the mind clears. Recognition itself can do the trick.

Sometimes the wandering of the mind is due to fatigue or lack of energy. There may be a physiological cause for it. Maybe you do not actually feel drowsy but, none the less, the energy for concentration is lacking. The art of it is to again and again recognise the state of the mind. If it is wandering, simply bring it back into focus. By doing this again and again, eventually the body energy will be renewed and you will have fewer periods of wandering thought. There is a daily cycle of energy. Within some periods you will have less than at other times. This is natural. There is no need for a fight. Simply be attentively aware at all times.

We can make use of an analogy here. Meditation is like using a fan – the old fashioned hand-held type. You have the task of catching a feather on the fan. Every time you move the fan, the feather is likely to be blown away. It is a delicate business. You have to hold the fan quite still just under the space through which the feather is sinking of its own motion. The feather then comes to rest on the top of the fan. You can imagine how difficult or how easy this may be! Any use of force and the feather is lost. Yet, once you grasp the principle it is something very easy to do.

Stilling the mind is like catching a feather with a fan. It needs patience and persistence. When practising, do not be afraid of a distracting thought. If your body has a problem do not be concerned with it. If your mind is worrying, put the worry down. Keep the mind on the method, waiting for the feather to sink onto the fan.

Supposing you are in a very good situation – no distractions, no wandering thoughts. Whatever you do, never congratulate yourself! Away goes the feather at once! So don't be happy! Do not think how successful you are. Just observe the situation without movement towards or away. If the mind moves, wandering thought begins.

Another analogy: some feathers come from chickens, some from ducks. Now the duck's feather is waterproof. A duck floats happily in water. No trouble! The chicken is a different case altogether. Imagine the state of the feathers of a chicken trying to swim! When we train, the mind begins with feathers like those of a chicken. It is easily disturbed by anything. But in time we find a state where equanimity appears and we are not bothered by any passing thought. At that time we have duck feathers! Of course, chickens cannot change into ducks but, through practice, the mind can become impermeable to the showers of passing thought.

> Protect the branches to save the roots;
> though a small matter it is not trivial.
> Close the seven orifices,
> shut off the six senses.

Here the branches are the minor vexations while the roots are the major ones that may last a lifetime. If one is not careful with the minor vexations they may develop into major ones. For instance, you may not be about to rob or kill anyone: yet, if the mind is filled by little hatreds or avarice, although you do not act upon these promptings, one day they may propel you to commit a crime. It is important to protect the mind from such a possibility. It means that not only do we have to be aware of how our minds function when meditating, we also need to be mindful in everyday life. When meditating you may put aside evil thoughts; but as you go about the world they may often assail you.

There are many examples of lives full of mistakes of this kind. Some people go into the mountains and practise, maybe for years. They come to feel that they have gone beyond all greed and hatred. The mind is calm so how could such negativities arise? They may even feel they have attained liberation. So they come down from the mountains and start interacting again in the world. Quite quickly they may get irritated by others or form some emotional attachments which they find they cannot handle. Greed and hatred appear and they are forced to recognise that they still have major vexations.

This result occurs because, even though hidden in the mountains and not experiencing any major trouble, still the minor illusions – the stuff of wandering thought – has not been put down. You can see how important it is to cut off even minor wandering thoughts. One who works hard with a method may not be able to cut off all illusory thoughts for all times. But at least he or she can get to the stage of cutting them off for a few seconds, minutes or hours. Even a few days. It is important to recognise that your mind can be free from illusion.

When such a person is faced with difficulty in daily life, it becomes easier to recognise the nature of that difficulty. Even as the vexation arises, the practitioner is aware of it and prevents a negative manifestation. But if one fails to practise after leaving the mountain, even though awareness may be present, a manifestation will usually occur. This is why many of us look forward to spending time in retreat or to practising in the mountains.

Closing the seven orifices – two eyes, two ears, two nostrils and the mouth – and shutting off the six senses – seeing, hearing, smelling, taste, touch and cognition – is the discipline of withdrawal from the attachments we have to worldly things. Such discipline in retreat enables us to perceive how the mind of illusion functions and provides a space in which clarity develops.

Wang Ming's poem may be causing some of us a problem. Simon the cook was puzzled when I praised the cooking at lunch time! Simon was worried that his good cooking might be distracting me from meditation! I told him that he need not stop cooking delicious food! A dish that tastes good, well, it just tastes good. The message is simply this, don't get attached to it. After you have finished, let it go. You never know, next time you could be disappointed. And the whole rigmarole of pleasure and disappointment gets going. Then your meditation is indeed disturbed.

When Wang Ming tells us to close the orifices and shut down the six senses, he does not mean that we should become senseless zombies, not seeing, hearing or feeling. What he cautions us against is perpetually wondering what kind of food we will have. Anticipation and disappointment create attachment and greed.

Once upon a time, when I was a young monk near Shanghai, I was with a group of boys who were so poor that we hardly ever had enough food. One day an old monk of better means provided us with some additional dishes. Amongst them was a plate of bean-curd. It was such a rare treat that one boy set aside a small slice so that he could relish it later on. He nibbled a tiny bit every day. For three days he managed to spin it out. But then one of our teachers saw what was happening. He slapped the boy and threw away his bean curd. The teacher told him, 'With this attitude you will end up as a Hungry Ghost!'

When we are engaged in meditation, our practice should not be suffused by attitudes of comparison. Maybe something is good looking, maybe something sounds bad. If it is so, leave it at that. We should act as if what we have seen we have not noticed, and what we have heard we have not regarded. We train ourselves so that the mind does not give rise to comparisons and illusory preferences triggered by the environment. Whatever we have experienced is simply so. There is no need to get worked up about it.

Perhaps you see a beautiful flower in the hedgerow. You like it, you pick it, you bring it home. Then it fades and dies. Maybe you forgot the water. Every day we hear the baaing of sheep and the bleating of lambs. When the animals are in the yard, there is indeed a great noise, like waves breaking on the shore. If you are truly practising, you witness the sound and nothing more. You will not be thinking 'Oh, how cute the little lambkins are! Oh, what a sad sheep that one must be! Perhaps it has lost its lamb.' Sheep are in the yard. That's all. When engaged in practice, you need not be concerned with them.

Pay no heed to forms;
Do not listen to sounds.
Listening to sounds you become deaf,
You become blind observing forms.

There is a deeper meaning here. When you listen to sounds you interpret them according to your nature. When you observe forms you likewise create a story about them. But these ideas you have are not the actual reality. The actual nature of the sound we do not hear. The actual nature of form we do not perceive. In that we do not perceive reality when we look at things we are as blind; when we hear things we are as deaf. Understanding the illusory nature of experience we should not get disturbed by whatever arises.

One of you has objected that if one lived as blind and deaf, one could not perceive the beauty of the world and could not experience gratitude for life. Pleasure and gratitude are related. Surely it is not wrong to feel gratitude?

Again it is important not to be mistaken about Wang Ming's message. We need to understand it with subtlety. He is simply saying that sentiments like gratitude have no place *within* practice. Before practice and after practice you experience the pleasures and pains of this world. Gratitude arises, compassion arises, love arises. It is in order to have a clear perception of the natural state that we need to practise without these things. The natural state is just as it is, naked, unintentional, unadorned by sentiment. We are speaking here of the vital elements of intensive practice where it is essential for us to have a mind of clarity. In everyday activity we experience the whole of life, including illusion. Through practice we can penetrate to the core and mindfulness can become part of everyday life too.

We are still in the state of the chicken feather. We do not yet perceive the meaning of the phrase in the Heart Sutra: Form is Emptiness and Emptiness is Form. In our practice, therefore, it is vital to investigate vigorously. In cutting off the senses we perceive mind without the intrusion of wandering thought. It is an essential aspect of training.

DAY THREE — EARLY MORNING

I have two themes for the day. These are:

Every Thought a Present Moment
Every Moment a Rebirth

As time passes, you witness the passage of thoughts. As thought succeeds thought, you experience the passage of time. In your practice it is important to make every thought the present moment. If you make yourself one with the moment, you stop the thought. There is simply experience without time because, without thought, time becomes a continuous present. You have to discover for yourself what being one with the moment actually is.

When you make every thought a present moment, there is no continuity of time, no carry over from moment to moment. Everything is continuously fresh, like the water of a spring endlessly bubbling up into the open air. In such practice every moment is a rebirth. Here we have no thought succeeding thought, rather there is endless re-creation, an endless momentless continuity. As one ancient master has said; 'One thought for a thousand years.' Yet, in this thousand years, there are no thoughts. There is simply a continuous unbroken newness.

This is why it is so important for a beginner to cultivate going beyond thought. Today, therefore, focus directly upon the present moment. There is no need to think about it. Just enter the present moment like a diver who has left the springboard. Plunge into it without judgement or consideration. When the diver dives, he lets go. There is only the long fall into the water, which takes no time.

Each time you sit down on your cushion dive into the present moment, becoming thoughtlessly one with it. And you will find that every moment is indeed a rebirth.

DAY THREE – BREAKFAST TABLE
REMARKS

In the USA there is a particular question which my Western trainees find especially important and which I would like to put to you here. In the Eastern tradition there is a major emphasis on no-self. It is no-self that has to be discovered. Yet, in the perspective of Western psychology, the most important thing is to develop one's personal self to a maximum degree, emphasising one's individuality, uniqueness and admirable qualities. One cannot get on in the world, it seems, without developing this assertive self. There seems to be a contradiction between East and West here. How can this be resolved?

Actually East and West are talking about the same thing but they are emphasising different levels. When we are young we have to develop our sense of personal identity in order to take on the world. If we don't know that John, Mary, Esmeralda or Harry was the name for this thing we call 'I', it would not be possible to relate conventionally with others, to pass examinations, to get a job; and since personal welfare depends on income and we need a livelihood, we have to function within that livelihood as individual persons. Which means we need to know how to manage ourselves in our relations with others. The Western psychologist is making a realistic point in stressing the importance of becoming an individual.

In fact without having a grasp of your personal identity, of who you are in the usual everyday sense, it would not be possible to train in Buddhism. The practice of Dharma starts with an individuality that has the will to train and practise the methods. To go beyond self there must be first a firm sense of self. Someone who is all over the place, who changes mood or intentions with every shift in circumstance, who has not been able to distinguish him or herself from others who are potent influences, is not equipped for the practice of Ch'an.

Yet wisdom comes from going beyond the elementary constructions of identity, from investigating who this is that walks, talks, argues and quarrels. When we go beyond, we develop a larger sense of self. A major step in this progression is the discovery of the undivided mind, one in which the splits produced by discrimination are healed. This is what I meant the other day when I spoke of the internal and external being united, or the body and mind becoming one. Yet the unified mind remains of the same structure as the divided one. It has not yet gone beyond. It is not the no-self.

What then is no-self? Look at the words. It is a state of being in which the self is absent. There is no self centre, no habit of self-reference. Everything else in experience is the same as before but the quality of being has become radically different. It is usually the case that the appearance of no-mind depends on the prior integration of the mind. So long as self and its object are separate, the one regarding the other, there is duality. The split mind of discrimination cannot transcend its own habits. You cannot experience release into no-mind from a divided mind only from a unified one. And where there is no-self we may say there is no-mind. For, in this perspective, the ordinary mind is the activity of self.

Practice therefore focusses on methods that unify the mind. We discover ourselves as whole beings through practice. Gradually, as we master the mental processes and bring about calming and integration, so we master ourselves. We gain control over the monkey mind. This wholeness is always a novel experience. Its discovery is a source of freedom, relaxation and clarity. It is the completion of the self as self. To reach this condition is already a major step. Most of us remain scattered in mind and body, discriminating and arguing within ourselves and with others.

Today is the third day. Let us attempt to integrate mind and body. This is the first step. Allow yourself to become one. Attain the state where body and mind are not separate in experience and then the external and the internal will also be united. Dive into your method wholeheartedly, without doubt or reservations.

DAY THREE – LUNCH TIME REMARKS

This morning I said two things. One was that every thought is a present moment; and the other, that every moment is a new birth. Time will not pass if every thought remains in the present. If every moment is a new beginning, time passes. If every thought is a present moment, can there be such a thing as time? Again, if there is time, can there be such a thing as the present? Yet, if there is no time, there is no present.

For us untrained practitioner it is impossible to be continuously in the present. It is therefore impossible for him to know that there is no time. Yet, so long as you are entangled by thoughts of past and future, the present is the best place in which to be.

For us who are beginners, there is time, there is past and future. And between past and future there is this present moment that we constantly try to capture; and, because of this attempt, every present moment is a new beginning. Since our minds are moving we are constantly starting afresh. Yet, when every present moment is a new beginning, there cannot be failure, displeasure or disappointment for these imply a carrying over of time.

Enjoyment follows the moment of pleasure but, so long as that moment exists, there is nothing to enjoy and nothing to be sad about. There is nothing intrinsically good or bad about each new beginning. One thing is simply following another.

When you are working in the kitchen and cut yourself by mishap there is a new wound. Your appearance is new when you buy fresh clothes. When you brush your teeth, even if the mouth is old, the teeth are newly brushed. Every day I find a new white hair. This is something new, a new grey-head is appearing. If we always know that every present moment is also a new beginning, a new birth, then there is nothing to be happy or sad about. It is simply that new collections of experience are appearing.

When I was a young boy, China and Japan were fighting each other. The whole country and my own village were very poor. In the old days it was the custom every New Year to wear new clothes and shoes. But in that year there could be neither new clothes nor new shoes. So I said to my mother, 'This year everything is old.' My mother said, 'Not so. Everything is new. The clothes are freshly washed. Trousers have new patches. Shoes are freshly repaired and cleaned.' That made me happy.

Whenever you practise, be in the present moment. Each one of them is a new birth.

DAY THREE – EVENING TALK

> Literature and Art
> are but busy gnats in the air;
> Technique and ability
> a solitary lamp in the sun.

Whatever our skill or learning, we should not consider ourselves extraordinary or our abilities special. There is a Chinese philosopher who said that whereas one's life is limited, knowledge is unlimited. How then can one be proud of attainments?

Intelligent people who are learned and proficient in complex disciplines or who practise skills in the arts often think of their activities as the most important in the world. They take pride in their accomplishments and look down on those less skilled. They have the habit of comparing the grandeur of their abilities with the mediocrity of ordinary folk. Doubtless such people are exceptionally talented but they would have great problems in the practice of Ch'an.

The accomplished academic, polished in his field and skilled in its discipline, tends to see everything through the perspective of learning. A scientist may see everything from the point of view of an exciting paradigm. A philosopher usually praises a certain school. The artist practising one style admires it more than others. All such tendencies are actually attachments to self rather than to knowledge. To have developed a skill becomes a mark of what one is and we defend it by superior attitudes, with pride. Such techniques and abilities are like lamps standing in the light of the sun. Being constrained by pride prevents one becoming one with the sunlight, extending one's mind to infinity. There is a fabulous bird with wings that extend from one horizon to another. In comparison gnats are insignificant.

Once when I was in Japan, I attended a Zen retreat. In the evening the master gave a talk. He spent two whole hours in scolding me, all because I had a Doctorate in Literature. 'What is the use of all this reading and scholarship?' he said. 'It is only an obstruction to practice. Such study only leads to arrogance, a bellyful of straw.' Afterwards I thought about it and went to see the master. I said 'How come you spent so much time scolding me?' He replied, 'If my words had not got to you, you would not have come to see me.' I had to acknowledge that this was indeed the case. Too much learning may indeed become an obstruction. At the beginning of this retreat John remarked to me that most of the participants were well educated and intelligent, and that this in itself could constitute a problem. Is that so?

> Those able and talented ones
> are really stupid fellows.
> Discarding the pure and simple
> they drown in too much beauty.

Those who consider themselves able and intelligent are actually foolish. You possess the seeds of wisdom if you think of yourself as a fool. A practitioner who experiences problems is doing well. One who thinks he has no problems really has difficulties! Of course, if you are enlightened, there are no problems. But, for those of us who have barely started to practise, it is important to recognise our problems, otherwise we are likely to have a troublesome time.

Often I find myself counselling practitioners who have lots of problems with vexations of body and mind. I tell them, if you recognise your obstructions, you are certainly practising well and with sincerity. Find out what you can do about your vexations. If you are stuck then come and see me. Eventually the difficulty will be resolved. If the vexation is the belief that you have no problems, that is sometimes a very difficult case! It is difficult for such a person to find the right motivation. Wang Ming tells us that if we can let go of our attainments and return to a pure and simple state then we can make progress. If not, there is trouble in store.

Practitioners of Ch'an should learn all kinds of skills, attain excellence in many disciplines. These things are the light of the mind and show us the breadth of our mental scope. They may also be the means whereby we can help others. Yet never mistake them for the unlimited wisdom. In these skills and attainments there is nothing reliable. If you are attached to them, then your intelligence has made you stupid.

> Consciousness is an untamed horse,
> The mind an unruly monkey.
> If the spirit is overactive,
> the body will sicken and die.

If you recognise the unruly monkey, then perhaps you can set about finding out what sort of wandering thoughts possess you. If you examine them you will find that rather than being of unending variety and interest, they are in fact few, limited in scope, repetitious and boring!

Maybe you don't know how many wandering thoughts you have, or what their nature is. They are like the sheep around here. Of course being good practitioners in the middle of a retreat, you have not seen them! But you probably saw them before the retreat started. To find out how many sheep you have, how many black ones and how many white, you need to be like the Welsh shepherd who rounds up his sheep with skilled dogs and corals them in a pen. Then, when they are all collected, he can count and examine them, give them names even. Whether you are like an untamed horse, an unruly monkey or a bleating sheep, the same principle applies. Be like the shepherd who rounds them all up. Then you can see what the problem is.

The problem is how to tame the monkeys. The first method of practice is to pen them up. You can do this by holding them in one place. You catch the thoughts as they come up and prevent them from wandering on. A device for doing this is the method of counting the breath. There are many variations of this method, depending on the unruliness of the monkeys. If the mind is quite concentrated, then all you need to do is to be aware of the breathing. You don't need to count at all. With a less concentrated mind, counting is useful since watching the breathing is insufficient to prevent wandering thought. If your mind is badly scattered, even counting the breath fails to focus the mind adequately. Discursive thinking keeps breaking through. So you make the task more difficult by counting the breaths in a reverse order, or by odd numbers and even numbers alternately. While the activity is simple, you give yourself more to do, so that wandering thoughts cannot gain a foothold. It is like tying the monkey to a tree after you have caught him.

The method of koan (kung-an) is based on a similar principle. It enables us to reach a point where we do not even have to concentrate. To begin with, using the koan is just like mechanically counting the breath. One repeats the koan over and over, like a mantra. As the mind becomes more focussed, you can use the koan in a more precise way. In Chinese this is called ts'an. It means investigation; looking into the mind to perceive its nature. When the mind is focussed you get a certain flavour from using the koan, and derive power from it. It is like eating ice cream on a summer day. It gets more and more attractive; and, as you immerse yourself more and more into it, wandering thoughts lessen. They may even disappear completely. However, this does not mean you are enlightened. It simply means that thinking in a random way has come to an end. The koan ties the monkey to the tree. You go deeper and deeper into it until you reach the point of Enlightenment. What is that? No explanation will help you. You must experience that insight yourself.

Although the koan method resembles counting the breath

at the beginning, it will take you all the way. This is unlikely through counting the breath alone. Even so, through counting the breath one can enter *samadhi* which is a valuable aspect of training.

Wang Ming says that if the spirit is overactive, the body will sicken and die. He means that if you struggle too hard with too much discursive thinking you will get very exhausted. Wild monkeys in a cage rush about destructively. You must consider the methods of training. To catch the feather you need to practise with a peaceful frame of mind, a gentle approach.

> Wrong conduct ends in delusion;
> Those treading this path become mired in mud.
> To regard ability as precious
> is called confusion.

You probably think that you must start climbing by going up, or that you must study to find wisdom. In the perspective of Ch'an this is inside-out thinking. Whoever seeks to climb ends up going down. Whoever seeks wisdom falls into confusion.

Where is the highest mountain, Karakoram or Himalayas? Let us say in the Himalayas. And where is the deepest part of the ocean? Maybe in the Atlantic or somewhere off Japan. We are lucky we haven't got an oceanographer here! We might discuss it all night. The more we know the more we find problems.

In our commonsense perspective, we say that the Himalayas are the tallest and the Atlantic perhaps the deepest. But if you go flying in a satellite then you get a different view. What then is high? What then is deep? Far or near, tall or short, big or small, these are all relative to the standpoint we adopt. 'High' to an astronaut is altogether different from what 'high' means to an inhabitant of Holland. Usually our mental scope is narrow and limiting. It is as if we create absolute values and scales with which to judge things. On the other hand, with a big enough mind, we do not attach ourselves to commonsense conceptions. We can contemplate with an unlimited range. From an earthling's viewpoint, however high one climbs is nothing compared to the altitude of the astronaut's experience. Divers who go deep in rivers cannot conceive of the depths of an ocean.

Knowledge is framed by our viewpoint. It is necessarily limited by the scope of intellection. If we spent a whole lifetime accumulating knowledge, it would still be like the mound of a termites' nest. It is not at all in the same dimension as wisdom. What then is wisdom? In the Ch'an perspective wisdom is a state that is free from attachments, free from measurement, free from self-reference and empty of vexation. It cannot be found through accumulation, through adding to a pool of knowledge, or through measuring how far we are ahead of others. On that path we only pile confusion on confusion.

In using the koan we usually focus on just one saying from the story. This saying is the hua-t'ou. We use it like a kind of lens to peer closely into the mind. Yet this is not an intellectual process. We are not saying, for example. 'Who am I?' or 'What is not?' or 'What is Wu?' in order to pile up descriptions or to elaborate theories. To ts'an the hua-t'ou means to look into it, to peer with the mind's eye rather than with the mind's reason directly into the moment of experience that is happening, right now. Description takes time, it accumulates, piles up; t'san has no time for it occurs in the durationless present. It is a bare looking into the space of the mind, like peering thoughtlessly into a goldfish bowl. There may be movement, sunlight glinting on the scales of fish, but there is absolutely no conceptual examination. There is merely the bare observation itself. It goes on and on. The hua-t'ou is, as it were, merely the target set up for you to aim at. Furthermore, although it may have the form of a question, the mind cannot make a quick intellectual reply. The usual sort of clever response is quite short-circuited. A fuse is blown somewhere!

Such looking generates a great doubt. The doubt becomes so intense that the mind automatically comes to one place, totally immersed in the paradoxical unresolvability of the hua-t'ou. You are lost in the hua-t'ou. When you are totally lost, that is ts'an. When this intensity of focus is long sustained, suddenly the whole mass of doubt breaks down, dissolves. That moment is Enlightenment. Nothing can be said of what is there then. It is beyond words.

There is also another method which I do not usually recommend to beginners. It requires a measure of prior practice. This is the method of the Ts'ao-tung school (Soto in Japanese), advocated particularly by Hung-chih Cheng-chueh in the eleventh century. This was the method favoured by the great Japanese Master Dogen, who took it to that country where it is known as Shikantaza. Actually, it is probably a very ancient method going back to the times of the Indian patriarchs. You might say it is ts'an without the hua-t'ou as a target. You sit gazing silently into experience as it arises. Hung-chih said of it 'In this silent sitting, whatever realms may appear, the mind is very clear as to the details, yet everything is where it orginally is, in its own place. The mind stays on one thought for a thousand years, yet does not dwell on any forms, inside or outside.' In this method, we let the mind go quieter and quieter, immersing itself in its own silence. It is like allowing the water of a pool to become utterly still. Every speck of mud drifts to the bottom and the water is crystalline in its clarity. This crystalline clarity becomes Enlightenment naturally and without effort. Like the method of koan, this is a wonderfully direct path. As you see, no knowledge, no attainment.

If I say any more there will be nothing to say tomorrow!

DAY FOUR – EARLY MORNING

This morning I have another three key words for you. These are:
Confidence
Vows
Compassion

The *Confidence* I am speaking of here is not simply a matter of self-assertion. This confidence is knowing at what level one's mind is working, knowing what situation one is in; and thereby knowing what one can do, or what it is one needs to do. It is the self-knowledge and the self-awareness that you have when you are mindful.

Confidence in Ch'an practice has three aspects. The first is the confidence that comes from mindfulness. The second is confidence in the Dharma and in the method of practice. The third is confidence in the teacher.

Confidence in the Dharma is what has brought you all here. You know the history of the Ch'an lineage. Many people have come to wisdom through the Dharma and through the methods of Ch'an. We need not labour the point.

Confidence in the teacher is often a problem. Each one of you has to find the teacher in whom you have confidence, and this depends on a sense of affinity. For example, this is the first time that most of you have met me. You have known me only a short while. You will not automatically have confidence in me just because you have heard others speak of me, or because you have read one of my books. We have to stay together for a while and get to experience one another in the retreat, in the interview, and simply as two people. If you find that being with me is in some way beneficial to you, then you will begin to have confidence. It is not necessary for the practitioner to know everything about the teacher, to speculate about his personality or his disagreeable or agreeable qualities. If there is this sense of affinity, confidence grows. Without this faith there cannot be faith in the method or the guidance.

The word *Vow* has the meaning of aspiration and determination. Without a vow to overcome vexation, the Buddha would not have come to Enlightenment. When he sat down at the foot of the Bodhi Tree he made the vow that he would not rise again until he had awakened. It was the strength of the vow that carried him through. The Buddha could see that sentient beings were in a pitiable state. He could have easily remained solitarily enlightened, but he made the vow to help others. Even earlier, when the Buddha decided to leave home and begin practice, his vow was not only for his personal benefit. Already he had seen the sadness of the world, of sickness, old age and death. He realised that if he could attain Buddhahood – liberation – then, and only then, could he be of real help to others. Without such attainment he could only be as a blind man leading the blind. His vow was not self-centred. It was large in scope.

Every morning, afternoon and evening we recite the Four Great Vows of the monastic liturgy.

> I vow to deliver innumerable sentient beings.
> I vow to cut off endless vexations.
> I vow to master limitless approaches to Dharma.
> I vow to attain supreme Buddhahood.

The vow to attain Buddhahood is the last of the four vows. The first is to help sentient beings. That brings us to the third word, *Compassion*. Compassion without wisdom is a sentiment coloured with emotion and attachment. This sort of self-concerned compassion may produce good acts but they will be within a limited frame. Do-gooding is often seen to be mistaken when the larger context is appreciated. The Buddha waited until he had realised wisdom before he began to help others.

In our case we should not wait so long. This is because we have the example of the Buddha before us. We have the teachings, the Dharma, as a guide. While we practise to attain wisdom, we may also practise compassion based upon the Buddha's teaching. Yet, if we rely only on the words of the Dharma and do not meditate and train ourselves in the Dharma, then our compassion will remain weakly based. It will not be the compassion arising within wisdom.

Let me repeat what I have said. If you do not have confidence it will be easy for you to get discouraged. If you do not have vows it will be difficult for you to persist in practice. If you do not have vows, when you find that you do not get instantaneous benefit from practice, you may regret it or think it is a waste of time. Without vows you lose determination. The vow to work for the benefit of all sentient beings is a great vow. It will help you to have persistence. Furthermore, a truly compassionate thought is selfless and will lead to the beginning of wisdom. In the Dharma, wisdom and compassion always go together, reinforcing one another.

From now on, every time you sit down to meditate, to practise your method, you should stand before your cushion and make the vow that on this occasion you will practise well. When sitting do not stir. Concentrate the mind within the method. Vow to penetrate the method before you rise from your seat. Vow that you will not abandon the sitting. Make a vow not to leave your seat voluntarily even if you collapse from bodily weakness. This is called making the vow to 'die on one's seat'. Of course, you are not going to die. Your body will ensure that. But if you vow not to get up until weakness overpowers you, then you will find remarkable strength. It is hesitation that divides the mind and makes for weak sitting.

We should know that in the whole world there are very few people who understand Buddha Dharma and actually practise it. The fact that we are practising together here means that we have good karmic roots. You may gain great confidence from this. There are so many people in the world who need help but if we do not practise we cannot even help ourselves, let alone others. When we practise with confidence and with vows, then wisdom and compassion mutually enhance one another.

DAY FOUR — BREAKFAST TABLE
REMARKS

During retreat the experience of time varies. The first three days drag by slowly. Each day may seem as long as a whole year. On the other hand, the last three days seem to run past like a swift horse. This is because, during the first half of a retreat, participants are neither used to the retreat nor to using their method; they have a hard time. During the second half, both body and mind are adjusted to the retreat and time seems to pass quickly.

Today is the fourth day. Do not think that there are only two days left and that, because nothing has happened in the first four days, you cannot discover anything. If you feel this way, then you may become lax in your effort and feeble in diligence. This would be regrettable and a great mistake. The retreat is like a race. Only when you cross the finishing line is the event over. You may manage a spurt in the last seconds and carry off the prize. But you are racing against yourself.

Practice with the method is like climbing a high mountain. You can only say the climb is over when you reach the summit. Perhaps you are climbing the mountain in a thick fog or a cloud. From the beginning, you have no idea how high you are. You may think you have come no way at all, and then you suddenly arrive. You may think you are nearly at the peak, and then you find further slopes rising before you. All you can do is climb. Without climbing you will get nowhere. In an act of faith you simply place one foot before the other. If you believe you are getting nowhere, you will become lax and the climb will exhaust you.

On retreat do not set yourselves particular goals for practice. Just keep going in the right direction. Every single step is then an act of reaching the goal. Going on is the goal. The goal is in the going. If you run a race and your mind is on the winning post you split yourself into now and then. If you forget the goal and just place all your attention on the energy of running, you will suddenly find yourself there. If the climber has his mind focussed on the summit, he may easily find the climb exhausting and stop half way, giving up.

In climbing a mountain, sometimes we encounter a steep slope. At other times we find a flat area to stroll across. The wise climber does not take particular notice of these differences. Both the steep slope and the flat area are high in the hills already. Likewise, when we practise, sometimes there arise good conditions and sometimes troublesome ones. If you find yourself in a good place, don't get too happy. There may be a steeper slope just ahead. On the other hand, in difficult times do not get discouraged; the slope will ease off shortly. On retreat you cannot predict one sitting session from the previous one. You simply have to sit down and find out. Every sitting is a new birth.

When climbing the mountain, you constantly experience differences in slope, differences in the demands made upon your energy and resilience. This goes on until the summit is reached. Similarly on retreat, do not be too eager for results. Take up an attitude of going forward without seeking anything. Use the ordinary mind to practise diligently.

People sometimes feel that all they ever encounter are the steep slopes. They never come across flat areas. Well, tough luck! You are tackling a steep mountain! When this is the case, you need to build stronger foundations for your practice.

DAY FOUR – EVENING TALK

To exaggerate clumsiness and covet skill
does not lead to great virtue.
Of much fame but little contribution,
their reputation quickly crumbles.

Many people suffer from feelings of inferiority. Others feel themselves to be very important; they exaggerate their self-respect into aggrandisement. Both of these feelings arise from comparing oneself with others. When you live alone you find that such feelings arise less frequently.

I do not know how modern psychology analyses these feelings but from the viewpoint of the Buddha Dharma each of these feelings is a different manifestation of the same basic inclination. A person who feels inferior is obviously lacking in confidence, but so is somebody who exaggerates his or her importance and behaves arrogantly. Both inferiority and superiority come from lack of confidence.

You cannot practise well if you lack confidence. You look at others and think how well they must be getting on. You feel as if nobody else has a problem; as if you were the only one sitting there worrying and anxious. Sometimes, when I find a practitioner is troubled in this way, I say 'Don't be so lacking in confidence! I too came by the same route. When I was young I also had to endure great difficulties in practice. It was only through hard work in applying the method that eventually I had a tiny bit of understanding.' Sometimes such a practitioner says to me, 'Shih-fu. How can I compare myself with you? You are a Ch'an Master, so how can I expect to get the same sort of accomplishment?'

Then there is another kind of person, not so common as the first, who may say to me, 'Shih-fu, you are now so old and I am young. By the time I reach your age I will definitely have surpassed you!' Such a person evidently has great confidence. But then, upon what is this practitioner basing his opinion? How can he be so sure? Actually, even with such confidence, there remains a big problem.

The first of these practitioners is putting him or herself down. There is a feeling of inability and inferiority. The second type is filled with arrogance. Of course, I shall be very happy if all my practitioners surpass me, but when practitioners show either of these attitudes, I am not so happy. Neither attitude is helpful in practice. In particular, a person who shows his lack of confidence through arrogance has very little chance of making progress so long as he thinks that way.

Now let me ask you, do you think it possible to be feeling inferior and behaving in a superior manner at the same time? Have you ever manifested such sentiments?

I see that many of us recognise such problems! The fact that we can perceive them is already a sign of progress.

If you know you have such weaknesses and yet still you try to cover them up and act as if you were truly confident, then you are like the praying mantis. There is a fable in which the mantis saw a carriage rolling towards it. It raised one of its legs to stop the carriage. Actually, it knew very well that such a thing was impossible but none the less it wanted to put on a show. The mantis is actually very pitiable. Such a pretence of ability is simply a manifestation of self-centredness.

Of course, there are also people who never try to resolve difficulties. They like to evade a difficult situation as much as possible. Such a person is like the ostrich sticking its head in the sand and hoping the lion will go away. The truth is that all of us are mantises and ostriches by turns, and we remain thereby in delusion.

In the Orient many people are like this. Perhaps it is the same in the West? Have you not met the man who is approaching thirty and begins to lose his hair. So, in case others should notice, he begins combing his hair in such a way that the hair on the left side goes over to the right! Yet, anyone who really takes a look can see at once that he is bald in the centre! Of course if you are a Ch'an practitioner and you are bald in the centre, well, you are bald in the centre.

A Ch'an practitioner needs to have this kind of self-knowledge. He should know what sort of appearance he has and feel at home in it. In whatever situation, you should know how far your ability will carry you. With the ability, you act; without it, you do not. No fuss, no pretence.

When I came to this retreat, I knew that many of you were well educated with degrees in psychology and other subjects. I did not think about it very much or trouble to look up these subjects in books and prepare myself for questions about this or that. I did not prepare myself at all in fact. I just came over. Here I am. I can tell you what I know. If there are things I cannot answer, so what! We can still talk together. The important thing is to recognise ourselves for what we are. Just recognise whatever you are, whatever abilities or inabilities you have, and accept yourself. There is no need to get vexed over comparisons. If you can manage this, you will become firm in character, more healthy and at peace.

Now let us look at the second two lines of Wang Ming's verse;

> Of much fame but little contribution
> their reputation quickly crumbles.

During an interview today one of you told me that he would like to help society. I said, well, in that case, you must finish your studies, get a reputation and some fame. Then you may be able to influence the course of social events. It is not wrong for Ch'an practitioners to become famous. If the reputation coincides with ability then there is nothing problematical about it. I myself have become quite well known. I have worked hard and have been of use to people. People have come to hear of me and this may perhaps be of value. More people may be helped as a result. If and when reputation and reality coincide, the truth is just as it is. On the other hand when a reputation does not coincide with reality but is simply the result of misleading self-advertisement, then there is danger. The empty arrogance of such behaviour can be harmful to others and deeply damaging to a person's progress on the Dharma path.

We can see that the four lines of this verse are connected. A person who feels inferior may be tempted to seek a reputation that goes beyond his or her real ability. This is arrogance based on weakness. It harms others and it harms oneself. Ch'an practitioners need to know their weaknesses. If you seek to correct them and do not try to cover them up, then you will become a more complete character and one whom others will trust. You do not have to become a saint, just a whole person in balance with yourself.

Suppose you were to meet two people, one of whom was over-praising himself and another who straight away said to you, 'Hey, look out, I'm a rascal! If you hang around with me you had better be careful.' Which would you prefer to deal with? The first may seem easier but the latter may turn out to be more reliable. Actually neither of these types knows himself well enough to behave genuinely. Neither the rascal nor the self-admiring guru needs to proclaim it. Their crumbled reputations have probably preceded them.

> Merely reading books
> is of no lasting value.
> Being inwardly proud
> brings the enmity of others.

What you get from books is merely knowledge. It is not your

own experience. An author only tells you what he wants to say. He has not written to speak to you in a current situation. Books are useful in setting a general direction, but you have to confirm what is said in your own way. Answers from books are mere descriptions. A book answer belongs to somebody else and not to yourself. In my own books, I have written at the beginning that they have been compiled mainly for my own benefit.

If you cannot find somebody near you who can be your teacher, then you can refer to books for some guidance. They give ideas about how to approach and solve problems. Yet, if you have only accumulated knowledge from books and not practised, then you are likely to think that you know a lot. Indeed I have met many scholars who have written about Zen. Often they do not meditate, yet they believe they are qualified to say all sorts of things about practice. This is really a vain claim. In actuality, they do not know what they are writing about. Such people often hold strong opinions and defend them proudly. They attempt to demonstrate that theirs is the only true appreciation of Zen by criticising others. They begin by describing how ancient masters actually had serious problems; then they take apart their own contemporaries. Such writers get involved in endless academic debates, increasing their pride at every exchange. If I say such people have problems, no doubt they will reply that I have problems too.

The best thing is not to compare. In attempting to prove your superiority you may only demonstrate the opposite. Sometimes a monk or layman may come to me saying, 'Shih-fu, I am sure you have high attainments in Ch'an. May I ask you this question. I have had such and such an experience. What do you think of this accomplishment?' I say, 'I am not you, so how could I know?'

Of course there are criteria for 'accomplishment', but I cannot use my personal perspective to judge another person. I am not that individual. All I can do is to respond to need. There is no benefit in confirming another person's insecurities. When there is no need for accomplishment, perhaps something has indeed been found.

> Using speech
> or written words
> to gain the praise of others
> is something most repulsive.

Ch'an tells us that we should not rely on words. Often it is better to say nothing. In Ch'an practice, the spoken and the written word is superfluous. Only a communication through a genuine mind is reliable. When old friends or family members have been separated for many years and meet again, what are the first words they say? Often there is so much that could be said that they cannot say anything. They just embrace or shake hands and that is enough. The contact says all the words.

Last year I went to mainland China for the first time in many years. I had not seen my brothers for thirty-eight years. So much had happened to them in that time. So much had happened to me also. When we met, we couldn't say anything. There were simply tears rolling down our faces. I myself was too embarrassed to cry, but tears were falling inside me and twisting my stomach. Everything was communicated just like that.

Legend tells us that Shakyamuni passed on the whole Buddha Dharma to the First Patriarch, Mahakasyapa, without saying any words. The Buddha was just holding a flower in his hand. Mahakasyapa smiled, and the Buddha said, 'That's it!'

In interview, one of you told me that his wife had said, 'I hope you will see Bodhidharma in Wales.' Well, I don't think I am Bodhidharma. If I were, I would probably spend my time facing the wall and not talking to you people! Would you like me to be Bodhidharma and yourselves to be the Second Patriarch in China? Hui-ko? If that's the case, then I must stop talking, turn around and face the wall and decide what to do! Ah, Richard is showing me his arm. Perhaps I should cut it off just as Bodhidharma accepted the arm of Hui-ko when he offered it in exchange for the teaching. Yet here that would be useless. Even if I cut off three arms it would not be useful now.

Actually you do not need to have Bodhidharma come to
Britain. In Britain you have Bodhidharma already. If you do
not understand this, treat it as a koan. Work on it.[1]

Wang Ming is saying that if you do not truly practise but
instead merely use the spoken or written word to tell others
about your attainment, then that is shameful.

In fact talking is useless. If people do not act upon these
evening lectures and meal time talks then these too are
useless. If people do not act, then this whole retreat, the
lectures, all the words, would be comparable to my bringing
a lump of clay from an Eastern mountain and dumping it on
a Western one. The propaganda of mere information is not of
use to you within your practice. Some may say, although
Ch'an speaks of no-self, the Bodhisattvas still teach compassionately to others. These are good teachings. Just to hear
them is good, and they should be handed on. So it is. Yet, I
say to you, without practice the teachings are not manifest in
the world.

DAY FIVE — EARLY MORNING

Today there are two important phrases for you
to bear in mind. These are:
Ordinary Mind
and
Wanting Nothing

The unbiassed content of the ordinary state of mind is both
natural and everlasting. To be natural, the mind needs to be
free from anything artificially created by thought or reasoning, from anything shaped by an experience or judgement.
When these things are absent we say the mind is in its natural
state. When the mind is natural it is in conformity with Tao.

Let me put it this way: here in the mountains in this old
farmhouse of stone and wood we are living close to nature.
Yet the tools we use and the clock that tells the time remain
man-made. They are not completely natural; but, for us, the

use of such simple tools is natural enough. It is of our nature to use such things. To wear clothes is natural and we feel comfortable. To take them off and be uncomfortable would not be natural for us, even if, at first sight nakedness might be nearer our original condition. Natural is what is appropriate. Natural is this: when there is one there is one, when there are two, there are two. Things are as they are. We do not need to add criteria of evaluation to fit our moods, thoughts or judgements.

Whatever is truly natural is everlasting; that is to say, the natural forms part of an unending timeless process which obeys unchanging principles. The sunlight from the window moves as a patch across the floor. It comes and goes as the clouds move across the sky. The sun itself follows its own unchanging route. The earth revolves on its axis so that we have the experience of the sunrise in the morning and sunset in the evening. The patch of light on the floor appears according to the rules of place, time and weather. All this is natural and everlasting. Water becomes rain and rain becomes water. This too is everlasting; it is of the eternal.

In the practice of Ch'an it is important to discover and to maintain the natural basis of the mind. If a practitioner remains with his illusory thoughts his mind is split; it does not come to rest in its natural state. Without discovering the natural basis, the practitioner sooner or later abandons his quest. He has not hit upon the eternal. Once the eternal is perceived, the practitioner is unlikely to give up, for he has discovered his own basis.

When we are born, the body-mind is in its natural state. Gradually we adopt unnatural contortions, defending ourselves where, if we were wise, we would find that no defence is needed. The practice of Ch'an enables us to go back to being natural, to rediscover the eternal quality of being. Every day we get up, wash, eat, go to the toilet – all this is natural. Similarly, we need to build into our everyday lives the practice of meditation. Let it be a natural part of daily life, not something special with a time set aside for it, but a quality of ongoing awareness.

When we look at the stream outside, we see the water

flowing. What is its purpose? There is no purpose. It is simply flowing. So let it be with practice. Practice itself has no particular purpose. If you give practice a purpose, then it is not natural practice. It is not rooted in the eternal. When your practice has no purpose, when practice itself is the purpose, then it is natural practice. Only this natural practice has the quality we call everlasting.

When your practice has no purpose, you are not seeking anything. You are wanting nothing. When you want nothing and there is nothing to want, what is there then?

Today is the last day. Please just use an ordinary state of mind to practise. No need for assumptions, moods, emotions, judgements. Simply follow your method. Work hard for no reason. Sit without any purpose in your sitting. Let the natural state arise everlastingly.

DAY FIVE — BREAKFAST TABLE REMARKS

The attitude we need to adopt in the practice of Ch'an is different from the attitude we take when doing work of other kinds, such as an academic study. Not only is it different; it should be quite the opposite.

Usually, when we are involved in a task that needs discipline or study we like to get on with the job, to get things done fast. If we hurry and get a move on, then we can get as much done as possible. If we hurry and work hard, then the result is usually proportional.

On the other hand, if you take a hurrying attitude in the practice of Ch'an you may achieve merely an undesirable result. If you try to hurry in calming your mind, the more hassle you will generate. If you hurry to get enlightenment, the more vexations you will create and you will be further away from your goal.

The practice of Ch'an involves training in patience, in determination. It requires the development of the will. The purpose of practice is to free ourselves from the self, to go beyond attachments to the self. If we are seeking rapid results, seeking to gratify ourselves in reaching some goal or some attainment, then this is the opposite of the purpose of Ch'an. If we get anxious because there appears to be no result from practice, we are making a mistake. In Ch'an, trying to make progress ensures no progress.

Let us return once more to the analogy of the feather and the fan. Before you can get any result from your practice you have to hold the fan in a very stable and peaceful manner; and if the feather does end up on your fan, it is important not to get excited. If you get too happy, there will be a slight stir of your hand and the feather will be gone. The question is, when will the feather drop on your fan and never fly away again? As long as there is an idea of attainment in which you imagine something and want it, the feather will keep floating away. In fact, the problem will last just as long as the feather and the fan exist for you. Only when there is no person seeking an attainment and no attainment to be realised will the ultimate solution arise.

DAY FIVE – LUNCH TIME REMARKS

During practice a lot of people find it difficult to distinguish between being diligent and being tense, between being lazy and being relaxed. In fact, the mind sometimes needs prodding, or even whipping, while at other times it needs comfort or consolation.

Applying the method has to be done skilfully. We have to learn through experience the skilful means of practice. If you feel tired or exhausted, it is probably because you have been sitting in too tense a manner. On the other hand, if you are dozing off and nothing seems to be happening, you may be too relaxed and becoming lazy. To find the right balance between tension and relaxation is not always an easy matter.

Sometimes you may find that you have become too tense. At such a time the best thing to do is to take a rest. Simply close the eyes and let the mind relax for five to ten minutes, not trying to do anything. It is important, however, to remain in the meditation posture. To lie down would be to lose all focus. Even though you have temporarily abandoned the method, you should not let go of the posture.

Sometimes you may become exceedingly sleepy. You may experience a dullness in the head which does not lift; or you may experience agitation and restlessness with the body shifting about and unable to sit still. In such a case it would be wise to break off from meditation altogether. You may go off somewhere, lie down and take a nap for half an hour. To do this you should leave the room. It would not be appropriate to lie down where other people are sitting. Find a place to rest and relax, take a nap until you recover your energy and focus and your mood is more peaceful. Then you can come back to practice.

In the first days of the retreat it is important to maintain the posture rigorously and not move about. There is now only half a day left for the retreat. The important thing now is to maintain the focus and peaceful quality of your mind. There is no need to drive the body too hard. If you are still having a lot of pain in the legs or back then adopt a less problematical posture. If you still have pain, you must none the less maintain a minimal amount of discipline. Do not move about too much because that will disturb others.

As the retreat progresses, some people can concentrate more and more effectively. But for others, an opposite tendency emerges. Their legs or back ache more and more and they find themselves fidgeting about a great deal. Again, this fidgeting may disturb others and it is important to create a time to relax and to become more peaceful. If you happen to be sitting next to a fidgety person, or even between two of them, then you should assert yourself and maintain the peaceful stability of your mind.

In this way, by discovering the skilful means for practice, you become mindful within the practice. You become able to maintain stability and peacefulness irrespective of disturbances within your body or in the room around you. Such training within practice has benefits in everyday life. You cultivate mindfulness and are less susceptible to the impact of others. You are not so easily thrown into laughing or crying fits or a bad tempered tantrum. Instead you maintain an evenness of awareness and are able to respond appropriately to whatever is happening around you.

DAY FIVE — TALK BEFORE PROSTRATIONS

In Ch'an we often perform prostrations. On retreat we do it together facing the Buddha. The monk sounds the handbell and we bow; he sounds the bell again and we rise from the floor. He sounds the bell again and we prostrate. So it goes on. We establish a rhythm of prostration in which all of us participate. You have been shown the correct methods of prostration according to the Ch'an school but there are some further remarks to be made before we begin.

There are several different reasons why a practitioner may wish to make prostrations. It is right that each practitioner chooses to bow according to the motivation of the moment that is of greatest importance to him or her.

The first reason for prostration is to pray. Why does one pray? Praying is common to many religions. Basically, one is praying for a response from the being to whom one prays. Here, whatever your understanding of the Buddha may be, you are praying to him for some benefit for yourself or for others.

The second reason is to express respect. We bow down mentally or physically to those we respect. We indicate an aspiration to emulate the respected one.

Thirdly, the practitioner may prostrate in order to show gratitude. We feel we have received benefits from the Dharma, from the Sangha and from the Buddha. It is impossible to pay back these debts, so we show our gratitude through prostration.

The fourth reason is to express repentance. We recognise that we have made many mistakes, said unkind things, lied, harboured harmful intentions towards others, entertained wicked thoughts, broken the precepts which we may have vowed to keep. Sincerely we wish to repent for all this.

Often, when the mind is confused, full of vexations and obstructions to practice, it is beneficial to prostrate again and again with the attitude of repentance. Each one of us has made our own karma. We are responsible for our vexations, even though we often wish to evade responsibility and attribute our problems to others. To bow in repentance is appropriate. When you bow in this way you come face to face with yourself, your weaknesses, the harmful mistakes you have made, even the wicked thoughts and acts you have committed. You do not try to avoid them as you make these prostrations. You do not cover them over and run away from such thoughts. Acknowledge and admit your faults and mistakes. Acknowledge your responsibility for your own karma. Recognise and seek to correct your weaknesses. It is with such an attitude that we do the prostrations of repentance.

The fifth way is to do prostration as meditation. In prostrating pay attention to the precise movements of the body. Make the intention and the action into one thing so that the state of body and mind is united. This method of prostration is valuable for those whose minds have attained a level of tranquillity which is stable.

This fifth way of prostrating can be done at several levels. The first is when you consciously direct your movements and pay attention to them. As you continue, this moves to the second level where you find yourself simply watching the movement. You are very clear about each movement of the body but you are no longer consciously controlling it. It is simply going on. The third level follows from the practice of the second. The body is now moving by itself, very slowly going down and rising up again. You yourself are no longer watching the body, you are no longer aware of yourself as a person at all. There is only the flow of movement.

So you may prostrate for praying, respect, gratitude, repentance, or meditation. The last is a prostration of the mind in which you allow it to move from the first to the third levels as it will. To begin with, the mind is controlling the movement; then the mind and body are moving together; finally the body is moving but the mind has become still.

Now each of you must decide which kind of prostration you are going to do. You make your own selection.

Now I will find a place for myself. Here will do.

DAY FIVE — EVENING TALK

Wang Ming goes on to tell us:

What common people regard as auspicious
the sage takes as evil.
The enjoyment gained is fleeting;
but the sorrow is everlasting.

Today is the fifth day of the retreat. By now some people have had some experience of the meaning of practice, and others may feel envious of their good fortune. From an ordinary point of view, such experiences are indeed valuable; but from an ultimate point of view they are not to be regarded as good. They are nothing special.

We have been talking about people climbing mountains. Some encounter easy flattish areas while others come across exceedingly steep slopes. We are pleased with the easy slopes and feel the mountain climbing is going well. But on the flat area the climber is not getting any higher! Someone struggling with cliffs and boulders on the steep slope may be on the quicker path. The climber wandering along on the flat area may be going around the mountain rather than up it! This is especially likely if he is climbing in a cloud.

Yesterday morning I said it was tough luck if someone seemed always to be on a steep slope. Actually, this may not be the case at all. Such a climber may be most fortunate.

Some years ago, during a retreat in the USA, I described the practice of Ch'an as like climbing a tall mountain. This mountain is made of glass. Furthermore, its surface is covered with layers of oil and grease. It is extremely slippery. If you try to climb it, there is no way you will not slide down! None the less, this is the task before you. The mountain is very tall but still you must climb. And still you slide down. This is the way Ch'an practice is.

In the end you discover that the glass mountain is an illusion; it has no real existence. One day when you climb up some distance and then fall right back to the bottom, you suddenly come to see that top and bottom are not different. Indeed they are the same. To understand this you have to become a climber. You have to make the effort to climb the slippery mountain. Unless you climb you can never know that top and bottom are the same.

Wang Ming is saying that for one who has never practised certain states and certain experiences are good and valuable. The sage, however, recognises that attachments to experiences or high states are a hindrance for they do not lead to liberation. The exalted states, the peaks, must also be put down. You have to go beyond this type of evaluation.

You may enjoy certain states or conditions and come to value them highly. It is like climbing up to a flat area with beautiful trees and running brooks. You arrive there and find it quite gorgeous. So you sit down saying 'Oh, how beautiful this is!' You forget about the climb. And next time you make the ascent, again you sit down in the comfortable spot. Perhaps you enjoy a snooze. In your dreams you are lotus eating.

Have some of you found such a place on the mountain?

The ancient Patriarchs cautioned their disciples about this, especially those who had had a first taste of Enlightenment. They told them that the road ahead was still very long. If you have only just begun to walk, then there is a long way to go. If you have had a glimpse of 'seeing the nature', then you have to practise even harder. Of course, when you fully understand, there is nowhere to go.

The danger is that people who have had a taste of Enlightenment confuse pleasing sensations with the real thing. They believe, 'That's it.' These sensations are perceptual experiences, mental responses or states, which are refreshing and give one a feeling of calm, peace or even a unity of body and mind. All these pleasing experiences have nothing to do with Enlightenment. They simply arise on the path.

At this point the wise practitioner should be very careful. Maybe you have come to experience the unity of the previous thought with the subsequent one. The experience is valuable. It is a sign of strong meditative practice. Yet this is not Enlightenment. Becoming one is becoming one, that is all. Yet, because it feels good, and because you do not know what Enlightenment is, you may mistake it for the real thing. So be cautious. Just continue without attachment to states that arise. As Wang Ming says such enjoyments are fleeting but the illusion might last forever.

Again, perhaps you have 'seen the nature'. You have perceived the emptiness of self in all things. You have experienced an awareness of the absence of self. You have seen the empty state where there is no-self because the self has vanished. You have had an initial taste of Enlightenment. You need no longer doubt it. Yet, as soon as you realise it and think about it, you are no longer there any more. When you speak of it, you are speaking of something past, a one-time experience. Such an individual is in danger if he then thinks he is enlightened. What was it? Now it is only a dead experience.

If you take this attitude there is no way you can make progress. Wang Ming tells us that if we have a good experience and hold onto it, evaluating it and wanting to repeat it, then we will have a very long night ahead of us.

> Beware of shadows and tracks;
> The farther you leave them the better.
> Sitting upright in the shade of a tree,
> neither traces nor shadows remain.

The shadows and tracks are the stimulations of the world. Some practitioners believe that the best thing is to shun society, stay remote from humanity in deep mountains or vast deserts. There is so much negative experience in worldly life. Actions of others, ideas, the need to rush, stress, confusion and politics all seem to offend. Better to leave them and go far away. Everyday life is full of problems: finding food, eating it, relationships, washing-up. It's all a heap of trouble. Much better to live simply in the hills. If this attitude becomes deeply engrained in you, it only takes you farther from the path.

The Buddha said that the Dharma is within the world. Enlightenment is not separate from the mundane. If you seek Enlightenment apart from this world, it is like seeking a rabbit with two horns. It does not exist. However, Wang Ming is speaking to beginners here. When you are beginning to practise, it is valuable to isolate oneself for a while. The shadows and traces are the retribution of previous karma, the negative features of the environment we have built up around us. This environment can be overwhelming. To isolate oneself is then valuable, for it enables us to begin to see clearly.

Here in the Welsh hills we have a secluded environment. Ricky here is an accomplished musician. We could ask him to play for us and to sing songs for us while we are meditating. While this might be fun, it would make progress in the practice very difficult. The wise beginner separates himself from such stimulation. In training, therefore, it is often wise to stay away from busy places.

Yet there will come a time when it is important to test the strength of one's practice. Then you must come down from the mountain and meditate at the crossroads. It becomes essential at some point to practise Dharma in the market place.

When you sit upright in the tree, neither shadows nor traces remain. But where is the tree? The tree may be either in the mountain or in the market place. In either case, you are surrounded by the retributions of your own karma. Yet, if the sitting is correct, then neither the shadows nor the traces will remain.

One day, during a retreat in Taiwan, I took the monks for a walk outside the temple grounds and into the town. After we had returned, one of the participants said to me that when he was outside he felt that while he was walking, the cars were not moving. When he had returned, he had the feeling he had never left. He felt inside and outside to be just the same. Time had not moved, although he had moved. Such an experience is valuable. Without it the monk could never have known that nothing actually ever happens in this world. Such insight is rare. Yet to stay in such an experience might be disastrous. You could be run over by the cars very easily!

> Worries of birth and distress of old age
> are products of your own thoughts.
> If the mind's thinking is ended
> Birth and Death are forever cut off.

One day when I was a young monk I met a very old and highly respected Dharma Master. Whenever he said anything, everybody listened to him with great respect. I admired him so much that I even envied him a bit. I said to him, 'I wish I could get older more quickly so that people would listen to me like they listen to you.' The old Dharma Master smiled and said, 'Well, yes, it is true that people listen to me nowadays, and it is about time they did so. I am about to die.'

In Buddhism there is a saying that monks should never be afraid of getting old, because when they are truly antique they will be treated like treasure. People think a monk has a deep practice because he has meditated for so many years, so they respect him and make him into a jewel. A wise old master might even receive a title 'National Treasure'! Naturally, once you are a National Treasure, you are very close to death. By the time everyone is listening to you, you will not have many days more in this life. To be afraid of death and to cling to life is actually useless. You have to appreciate that birth and death are not two separate things. The day you are born you are already starting to get closer to death, moment by moment. With birth there is always death. Birth implies death. Only when there is no birth can there be no death.

The Ch'an practitioner must come to realise that wandering thoughts and illusory intellection are the very stuff of birth and death. Only when illusory thinking is cut off completely will there be no more birth-and-death. When all illusory thoughts of self-perpetuation and the vexation that such thoughts maintain are finally cut off, all that is left is wisdom.

Wisdom means the comprehension of Emptiness. In Emptiness, all comings and goings are seen to be aspects of the same process; the interdependent origination of all things. Coming and going, birth and death, are not separate. They are one. To be afraid of death is to maintain illusion. The question is, can you, the practitioner, practise to the point where illusory thought and vexations are cut off?

We cling to life. We are afraid of death. This is normal, for we want to stay young; we do not want to grow old. Of course it is impossible. Even if you do not want to die, eventually you will do so. Thinking of these events in time attaches us to the products of time. It is the thought that generates the pain. In our practice we go beyond thought into the continuous present. As you enter that sphere, all fears of birth-and-death, of moment-to-moment, of one thought following another, are completely cut off.

Somebody once asked me, 'Shih-fu. Supposing I were to listen to you and practise very hard but, before I managed to cut off all my illusions and vexations, a plane crashed on my house and killed me, what would happen to me?' I answered 'In that case, you would probably become a practising ghost!'

My answer was not very serious. Indeed it was a Dharma joke. In the Buddha Dharma there is a different view. If you have practised diligently all your life, you have established a direction for living. This direction becomes part of your karma. In your next life the tendency will continue. You will go on moving forward to the place where illusory thought disappears. It is like a tree to which a rope has been attached so that it leans in a certain direction. Suppose the tree is being pulled towards the east. Then, season after season, when it puts forth new growth, it will continue to grow in an easterly direction. When eventually it is cut down it also falls towards the east. It is important to set a direction in life. As I have already said, the practitioner needs to have confidence, yet without vows that is not enough. The vow that is the intention to practise gives a direction to your life and produces new and beneficial karma.

> Not dying, not born,
> without form or name.
> The Tao is empty and tranquil.
> The myriad phenomena are equal.

In the Ch'an perspective to say no-birth and no-death does not mean that you are not born into a cycle of birth and death. The writer of this verse has perceived that there is no particulate reality to either birth or death. These events are not things, but merely moments in a great continuity. Centred within this mutual arising of causes and conditions, the ideas of birth and death no longer produce separations into beginnings and endings. These names and forms no longer make any difference. For such a Buddhist sage, even though he is within the cycle of birth and death, he is liberated from it.

In the Hinayana tradition, liberation means the transcending of life and death, the movement from Samsara to Nirvana. In Mahayana, and therefore in Ch'an, the meaning of liberation is different. Even though a practitioner or a Bodhisattva is in Samsara, he or she does not consider Samsara as suffering. For such a person, liberation means that even in Samsara he is liberated from Samsara, he is free to come and go. To the Bodhisattva, birth does not have to have the form of birth, nor death the form of death. Both are seen to be aspects of a greater whole – so what does it matter?

'The Tao is empty and tranquil, the myriad phenomena are equal.' The word 'Tao' refers here to the condition of continuity within which birth and death are one. To a practitioner who perceives that birth and death are one, whatever life and death may be is no longer of concern and, being without vexation and wanting nothing, everything appears equal within a vast tranquillity.

The Bodhisattva is attached neither to staying within the cycle of birth and death nor to leaving it. Samsara and Nirvana are all the same to him. He is no longer focussed upon his personal needs. Indeed, if the Bodhisattva still had a sense of self-concern he would not be truly liberated. With no self-concern, he views the world and sees the sufferings of the myriad of peoples. As the Bodhisattva looks down so great compassion is born. It is a compassion rooted in the total absence of self-concern.

A Bodhisattva neither has anything specific to do, nor anything that he does not have to do. He or she does not aim at a particular target. Sentient beings manifest suffering within many causes and conditions. It is to these conditions that a Bodhisattva responds. In this caring for sentient beings the Bodhisattva does not discriminate one from another, choosing to help one and not to help another.

Sometimes a practitioner may ask, 'If the Bodhisattvas have so much wisdom and so much compassion, how is it there are still so many suffering sentient beings? Do the Bodhisattvas look after some and neglect others?' In the scriptures there are two parables about this, two sayings. In the first, compassion is likened to rain. It falls on everything and does not discriminate. Yet large trees get a lot of water and small trees in the shade of the larger get less. The rain is not selective, yet there are conditions in which it cannot be received. In the second, compassion is likened to sunlight. Just like the rain, sunlight is universally giving. It neither selects nor does it discriminate. Yet a blind person cannot see the sunshine. A prisoner in cellars cannot see the light. Karmic conditions from one's own past determine whether one can receive the benediction of the Buddhas. For this reason, training is necessary. We cannot depend on the compassion freely given by others. We have to do our own work. We have to find out what that work may be.

> What is of value? What is cheap?
> Where is there shame or glory?
> What is excellent or inferior?
> How can there be heavy and light?

When the meditator comes to understand that there need not be discrimination; that the whole process of discriminating is a matter of illusion; that, although things exist conventionally as they are, yet they need not be taken as fixed entities; then a fresh sort of vision becomes available.

When we describe things, we usually do so in dualities

based upon our attachments; things are good or bad, tall or short, big or small. These are the words we use to manage our practical concerns in the world. When we deeply investigate (ts'an) these conventions, we see that we have allowed them to bind us into a prison of words. There is an infinity of opposites and comparisons. For one with Dharma insight, such discrimination appears as arbitrary. If there is no longer anything to gain or lose, then everything is experienced as equal within the endless arising of causes and conditions. This is simply the nature of being.

> The clear sky puts purity to shame.
> No brightness compares with the brilliant sun.
> Stable as Mount T'ai,
> Steady as a golden wall.

What else can be added? There is no need to say more.

DAY SIX — EARLY MORNING

This is our last early morning meeting together so I would like to leave you with two sets of principles; the first for your practice of meditation, and the second for your everyday life.

When you are meditating, the three principles to bear in mind are:

> Regulate the body.
> Regulate the breath.
> Regulate the mind.

When you sit it is important to sustain the correct posture. This is most beneficial for the whole practice. Sitting correctly is good for health; it can even cure certain problems. The legs should be in either the lotus or the half lotus position. However, if these positions are too difficult for you, then there are other approved postures that you may use. Doing some yoga to make the legs flexible is much to be recommended, especially for beginners who find sitting uncomfortable. The back, neck and head should be vertical but not strained. The mouth should be closed with the tip of the tongue touching the upper palate. The hands should be held in the lap with the fingers joined in the proper way. Usually you should keep the eyes open and directed downwards at about forty-five degrees to the horizontal. Once you have adopted a correct sitting posture, you should make sure you are not sitting tensely with the muscles under strain. It is important not only to hold the correct posture but to do so in a relaxed manner.

The breath should be smooth and natural. It is not necessary to control it in unusual ways. Just notice the breath flowing in and out through the nostrils. After some time, move on to observing the breath as it reaches down into the abdomen, noticing also the slight movement of the abdomen itself. Once you have focussed for some time on these movements, let the centre of awareness simply come to rest in the region of your navel.

Once the body and breath are regulated, the mind will gradually settle into a calm state with few wandering thoughts. The mind follows the breathing into a natural relaxed state. When the breathing becomes naturally deep, long, fine and subtle, so also does the mind assume these characteristics. Yet, you must remember not to seek to control the mind in order to reach this goal. The mind needs to be allowed to settle naturally. If you contort your mind with excessive efforts, you only produce vexation.

The three principles for everyday life are:

> Be mindful of your words.
> Be mindful of your actions.
> Protect the quality of your mind.

We have spent a whole week examining a text on calming the mind and observing the importance of letting go of wandering thoughts. We need to control this mind of illusions through letting it become calm. It is this that allows us to understand non-attachment. In your daily life it is important therefore to maintain the practice of meditation to protect the quality of your daily awareness. Too much talking without reflection can be harmful. It maintains a noisy mind; it releases our wandering thoughts in a mutual contamination so that we harm rather than help one another. Of course this does not mean we should always remain silent. It means we need to be mindful of what we are saying and not open the mouth and just let it all out. Mindfulness of what we say sustains clarity and makes our interactions with others pure also.

Similarly, we need to be mindful of our actions. It is natural to make all sorts of bodily movements – hands, legs, feet. Like all animals we do so from morning to night. Yet we need to make these actions in a manner that is natural; that is in accord with the criteria of the society in which we live, and which respects things beneficial to the self. If we do not behave in these ways, we damage ourselves.

The practitioner who has freedom of body and mind through following natural principles will always behave in ways that are beneficial both to self and others.

At the end of a Ch'an retreat in New York I usually hold a simple ceremony in which we affirm our adherence to the Five Precepts. If we hold these precepts, we naturally follow the three principles of meditation and the three principles of daily life. However, here you are not all of the same background and have not necessarily taken the Three Refuges of a Buddhist. Some of you may hold religious or non-religious principles that may seem to conflict with some aspect of the precepts. This would cause unnecessary difficulty and raise needless vexation. So this time we will not hold such a ceremony. Instead we should meditate upon the six principles I have just described to you. If you live according to these principles you will find out for yourselves the nature of the benefits that follow.

DAY SIX – BREAKFAST TABLE REMARKS

We are coming to the end of our retreat. For me coming to Wales has been a rare opportunity. I would like to leave behind everything I know about practice and to offer it to everyone here. Those few of you who have done a retreat with me in New York will know that I usually only give talks in the evenings. Here I have been speaking in the early morning, at breakfast time, at lunch time, nearly every day! This is because I am unlikely to be able to come here again and I feel the need to convey as much as I can right now.

I am like some merchant who goes from market to market with a large bag. I set up my stall, tip everything out and put it on view. If there are buyers, well and good. If not, I stuff it all back into the bag at evening time and go on my way.

At this market place in the hills of Wales, you all went through a lot of trouble getting here and making preparations, and for a lot of that time you were not even sure that I would get here! Now we have done six days' hard work together and we are going home saying there is nothing to seek and nothing to gain!

Sit-at-home people say that mountain climbers are really wasting their time. They have nothing better to do, so they try to climb mountains, tire themselves out and come back with nothing to show for it. Yet the person who climbs a tall mountain sees a world and experiences nature in a very different way from one who never leaves his own front door. Genuine mountain climbers do not struggle up the Himalayas for the honour of it. Honour is bestowed by others. A true climber climbs simply for its own sake; he climbs for the experience of climbing. And this is an experience no one can have without setting foot upon the path. This is true even if the mountain is a glass mountain covered with ice and you never get more than a little way nearer the sky.

If there is any purpose to Ch'an, we may say it is to discover the nature of the self and the world that appears to self. Those who make this effort discover something sublime. They do not do it for the honour, for praise from others. In investigating the nature of self they may go beyond it to somewhere which cannot be described.

Even so, these Ch'an climbers are of many sorts. Some try to climb the glass mountain for their health! Some prefer tall mountains, some like shorter ones. Some are not even concerned about reaching the top. They just like to go a certain distance every day and if they find a small hill then that will do. Some like crossing passes into unknown valleys where the people speak languages they do not understand; perhaps they begin a new life there. Of course the higher one goes the further one sees, yet the quest for the longest view is not the only quest. Your quest is set by your karma. The true quest is the koan of one's personal life. Nobody's life is like that of another; we each have our own mountain, our own way on the mountain. Whether you are aiming for the top, or just need to go a little distance to the crest of the nearest rise; in either case the journeying brings benefits.

So, regardless of the reasons which brought you to this retreat, to have practised here is better than having not practised. To practise diligently, to put time, energy and concentration into it, to understand the meaning in the method, all these bring benefits that may be hidden from you now. For the remaining time here do not let go of your method. Maintain your focus.

When you go home, try to maintain a daily practice and, when you find the opportunity, come again to an intensive retreat. The more effort and time you put into practice, the more you will come to realise. Even if right now, after you have spent five days sitting patiently here, you feel you have not 'gotten' anything, by the time you go home you may feel differently. When you are once more in your own house you may recognise the difference. You are not the same as you were six days ago. You must find this out for yourselves.

CLOSING CEREMONY AND FINAL WORDS

When you have received something, it is good to be aware of from where it has come. If you take a drink of water, it's good to know the source of the water. Perhaps it comes from a lake or a river. Should you want to drink again, you will know where to find it. If you have not noticed where something comes from, you are like a man who crosses a bridge and knocks it down behind him. He can never return or make use of it again. When you know where something comes from, you can be grateful for the source. Gratitude is part of wisdom.

Of course the river flows spontaneously and without conditions. The water does not mind whether anybody is grateful for it. It doesn't mind whether anybody remembers where their glass of water came from. It is we, who need the water, who would be wise to remember the source of the water and to be grateful. If we fail to remember the source, then, when we need some urgently, we may be forced to dig a well – which may be too late.

During this week we have received the guidance of the Three Jewels, the guidance from the methods of practice and the opportunity of being here to participate in this retreat. We should now express our gratitude for these things.

To whom are we grateful? First, we should express gratitude to the Buddhas of all times and of all quarters. We should show gratitude to the Patriarchs and the teachers of previous generations who, together with generations of practitioners, enabled the Dharma to be transmitted. We should offer thanks to our parents and to all sentient beings – to whom in one way or another we are related – for their help. All these things have made up the set of conditions which enabled us to have this opportunity to practise.

The ceremony is simple. I will express our gratitude and then after each line we will make a prostration. Please join your palms.

We express gratitude to all the Buddhas of all times and all quarters.

We express gratitude to the Dharma of all times and all quarters.

We express gratitude to the Sangha of all times and all quarters.

We express gratitude to our own teacher and master Sakyamuni Buddha.

We express gratitude to all the great Arhant disciples of Sakyamuni Buddha.

We express gratitude to all the Patriarchs in each generation who have lived in India, Tibet, China, Japan and other countries.

We express gratitude to Bodhidharma, the first Ch'an Patriarch in China, who brought Ch'an from India.

We express gratitude to the Patriarch who completed the Chinese Ch'an teachings, the Sixth Patriarch Hui-neng.

We express gratitude to the great contemporary master Hsu-yun of whom Shi-fu is a lineage descendant, and also to Shih-fu's personal teachers Master Ling-yuan and Master Tung-ch'u.

We express gratitude to our parents and all sentient beings who have helped us.

We express gratitude to this teacher who has guided us and been with us this week.

Finally I would like to express my own gratitude to all of you who have helped each other complete this course and in bringing about the causal conditions that enabled me to bring this Buddha Dharma and Ch'an teaching to Britain. A further step in the transmission of Dharma to the West has been made. For this I am infinitely grateful. Let us prostrate together.

There are now just a few final things to say. I myself do not have great practice. It is simply that I left home when I was thirteen years old and now that I am sixty-one I have had forty-eight years collecting some experience of Buddha Dharma. I have come to realise how great and how good this Dharma is and how very few people truly appreciate it. I am just an ordinary person exactly like everyone else here. I am not a Buddha. All I am doing is trying to apply what I know in order to help others. It is not I who helps others; it is the Buddha Dharma that is helping people.

Yesterday morning I said I felt like a travelling merchant who goes to far-off places carrying a bag of wares. In this distant place I would like to open my bag and leave everything behind. Then I can go home empty handed, at ease and happy.

Whether the things I have brought here are useful to you people or not is for you to say. If it has been of use, naturally I shall feel grateful. But the bringing of the Dharma here is actually not for any purpose. It has not come for any reason at all. The Buddha Dharma itself is the purpose. So in bringing the Dharma here I am not asking for anything in return. I would like to suggest that you adopt the same attitude. Each of us can bring the Dharma to him or herself through training and then reveal the benefits to other people. Very often in the teachings we are asked to express gratitude to the Buddha and the Three Jewels. But Buddha is already complete, perfect. He does not need anything from anybody. The best way to express our gratitude is to reveal the benefits of the Dharma to everybody, to every sentient being.

When Sakyamuni Buddha was about to pass away, his disciples asked him, 'Buddha, after you have passed away, upon whom can we rely?' The Buddha replied 'The teachings that I have given you for some forty years, that is the Dharma upon which you should rely.' You too should rely upon the Dharma, the Precepts and your own efforts, and not upon the teacher. Of course, if there were a great Ch'an master who came to Britain that would be good, yet whether there is a Ch'an master in Britain or not is not the crucial matter. So long as people have a good understanding of the Dharma and practise accordingly, benefits will arise. Even if I were to come here every year until I was a hundred years old, it would only be at certain times that the Dharma was practised. The Buddha Dharma is eternal and ever present. This person Sheng Yen is of no importance to you. The vital spark is the teaching that he leaves behind with you. And this Dharma is not my Dharma. It is the Buddha Dharma of Ch'an.

NOTES

---

1. Does anyone want to have a go at it? See Model Subject No 1 in the Hekigan Roku (*The Blue Cliff Records*, translated by R. D. M. Shaw, 1961, (Michael Joseph, London), the major collection of

koan cases. Bodhidharma came from the West and the devout
Emperor Wu, who had built many temples, interviewed him.
Bodhidharma was not impressed by temples, so Emperor Wu
asked him for the first principle of Buddhism. Emptiness not
sacredness, said Bodhidharma. The Emperor was offended and
could not understand. Bodhidharma crossed the river and was
not seen again. Hadn't he gone off to a cave somewhere? So
what purpose was there in his coming? Could he not have given
the Emperor more appropriate instruction? Why cause such a
disturbance? What is the difference between the sacred and the
empty? Where has he gone and how will he appear again?
Wherever the cool breezes blow from nowhere to nowhere
there may he be found. So what can you do about that – now –
in this country? Shih-fu came here out of the West. Or was it
from the East via New York? Why stay so far out on the
periphery of the compass? See also, Sheng Yen, 1990, *Ch'an and
daily life*. (Ch'an Newsletter 78, May, p. 3 (ed).)

2 PROBLEMS IN THE MINDS THAT SEEK THE WAY

Participants' Experience of Ch'an Retreat

HOW DID did the participants at the Ch'an retreat experience it? To answer that question Shih-fu always asks each participant to write a brief report within a few days of the ending of a retreat. In Wales he made the same request and in due course received a number of descriptions. These accounts provide details of the difficulties and joys that people experience in Ch'an practice and, since others may find them instructive, I have edited a number of them for the readers of this volume.

Each report has been extensively pruned to preserve the anonymity of the contributer and to bring out the essential focus of concern. The essence of each report is the light it throws on the structure of the individual mind seeking enlightenment; for it is this very structure that constitutes the basis of the vexations that plague that mind. This karmic basis is the mental conditioning of an unique ego that endlessly and in a bewildering variety of ways seeks to preserve itself against the abandonment of self that fore-shadows enlightening experience. To 'put it all down' is the task that each individual faces – just as it faced Master Sheng Yen himself in his encounter with his teacher (p. 115).

In each report, it is of interest to uncover those barriers, often taking the form of still unconscious self-assertions, that block further insight. Clearly, within the practice of Ch'an, intellectual analysis of these delusory identifications is not helpful, but mirroring comment in interview often leads a

practitioner to a new perception and hence to the possibility
of letting them go. In this presentation, I offer a few intuitive
comments after each report as a probe in this direction. We
hope they have a useful function in giving the reader a view
of the methods of instruction available in Ch'an.

1. *Medical practitioner. Male.*

I took little time in making up my mind to apply for the
retreat. After all, who could resist John's enticement to
experience 'the real thing'? I came to the Maenllwyd on my
48th birthday, a bit angry and inevitably deflated by the news
that Shih-fu had been prevented from coming. I had told my
wife that I had a strong feeling he would be there, and, since I
don't trust these bouts of intuition, finding him sitting by the
fire was the best birthday present I could have wished to
receive.

The week was not an easy time. This is not to say that I
didn't gain something immeasurably precious and inspiring –
I certainly did; but pain was my main concern during these
six days of intense self-confrontation.

Knowing cushions would be provided, I had left my
friendly stool at home. How I wished I had been told I could
bring it. I soon developed pain in my right leg, from buttock
to foot, which was unrelenting whatever support I assembled
in a desperate attempt to prevent it. The annoyance and
frustration were intense, and I was in despair. How could I
retain the small gains I had made in my ability to concentrate
on my own at home? How was I to learn new depths of
meditative experience, when all I was doing was thinking
'How can I go on with this pain?'. By day three, I acquired
a knack of directing my attention away from the pain, so
that it seemed to change to heat instead. Even so, the
awareness of it never departed. Towards the end of the week
I found I could begin to concentrate better only when the
pain had reached an intense pitch, and I was able to apply my
'knack'.

I found our visits to the field for walking a delicious break in the sitting programme, and was able to 'pay attention' to my feet rather better than to the wall. My depth of concentration was nothing extraordinary, simply a luxuriation in the softness of the earth. The no-thinking looking-and-listening exercises were also helpful, and, as the week waned, I repeated these on my own in an increasingly desperate search for a 'peak experience', knowing at the same time how hopelessly useless my striving was. I somehow craved for reassurance that *I*, too, could 'make it'. Seemingly, the door was closing in my face. I wept bitterly. Somehow I fought against all we had been told – that it is useless either to expect or to strive for 'results'.

This intellectual pain, if I can call it that, was also hard to endure. The adamant refusal of my monkey mind to quieten down made me begin to believe in the Devil! It even interrupted one hard-won stillness with the anouncement, 'My mind's now still'! This gave rise to further despair.

Since I am always suspicious of things I cannot understand, the religious devotions caused me a problem. Shih-fu's homilies were always totally inspiring because they were so crystal clear and obviously trustworthy. The liturgy of the Buddhist devotions, however, was to me strange and obscure, and I found myself fighting it. It was helpful to be reassured that it didn't matter that I had no feeling of devotion to Buddha and his successors; that it was all meaningless anyway; that it should be regarded as a meditation. The resulting abandonment of judgement allowed me to experience at least some feelings of emotion. The prostrations were especially exquisite in the intensity of distress they produced when performed for repentance and prayer.

How necessary is this religious aspect to my progress up the mountain? Surely, the realisation of human potential in the ultimate service of others is an essentially secular endeavour. I can understand why respect should be accorded Sakyamuni Buddha and his successors but their elevation to an apparently divine status seems contradictory, though doubtless of inspiration to the faithful.

Emotional pain coloured my week as it wore on. My disappointment at the poor quality of my sittings turned to despair as the days went by. I started by watching my breath, but had arrived at the retreat hoping that Shih-fu would 'promote' me to a 'superior' method fairly quickly. I had formed the impression that breath-watching was kid's stuff, and that serious practitioners of Ch'an soon moved on to better things. As my inability to concentrate lessened, I checked to see if I was due for 'promotion'. I was excited to be allowed to adopt 'Silent Illumination', but this change of method seemed to deal a fatal blow, and thoughts intruded once again with renewed clamour.

These distracting thoughts were largely self-centred. I found myself increasingly concerned at the impression I was making on others and on Shih-fu. I invented ridiculous fantasies and posturing, in spite of a knowledge that everyone was far too occupied with their own task to be paying any attention to me. This acute awareness of how much I look to others for approval I found to be very painful; doubly so by not being 'allowed' to reason it through because of the 'no thinking' rule. I constantly searched for the 'real me'; something which I seemed to have lost.

My other preoccupation consisted in a distressed search for the reason for my incessant thoughts. Do I rely on my powers of reasoning as my 'passport' in life? The culmination of despair occurred on the final evening before the 'discussion'. I had a feeling of total failure. I had so wanted to succeed with the Ch'an/Zen approach, to realise my potential as a human being; I felt somehow the door was being slammed shut in my face. What was it that I lacked that others seemed to have? This despair led me to judge the week with a purely emotional yardstick. In spite of arguing with myself to the contrary, I realised that I had come to the retreat with huge and hopeless expectations, and had become disillusioned when these didn't materialise in the way that I had hoped.

Today, as I write, I realise I have received an immense treasure of wisdom and teaching; of having been personally helped, consoled and inspired by someone who seems to understand experience supremely well and who realises what it is to be fully human, and to use that knowledge compassionately for the benefit of others. I could not aspire to anything greater.

Comment
Such an effort to get things right! Sheer will develops too much expectation unless balanced by greater ease. Putting oneself down makes it difficult to get up. What is meditation for? To feel better about life or to understand the self? Why create a difference between the secular and the religious? Dropping the opposition of categories would be a way forward.

2. *Young musician. Band leader. Male*

Before arriving at the retreat, I had been experiencing a lack of balance in my life. My emotions had been extreme like a fire burning its roots. On arrival I was anxious about everything. Where was I to sleep? How was I going to return home? I asked myself this no less than fifty times in the first two days!

To begin with my concentration was very bad. I was constantly looking forward to the next meal or the next talk. I entertained feelings of wanting to leave, was generally distracted with a lot of pain in my body. The exercise sessions were vital. During the first days they helped to maintain my morale and body energy. Shih-fu's teachings were entertaining and enjoyable, but also deeply threatening. It seemed that if I had to cast off the past and future, I would be casting away everything that I loved. It filled me with sadness and grief. A thousand thoughts of past pains and future hopes flooded my mind saying, 'You can't throw us away – we are you!'. But, somewhere in me, I understood the freedom that was being held out to me.

My first interview with Shih-fu was very short, I told him about my emotional state and the pain I was feeling. He told me that my Chi was rising too much and that, when I felt this way, I should think about the soft part of the sole of my feet and the pain would go. I followed his advice and it worked so well that I found myself trying to will the pain back thinking, 'This can't be so easy!'

During the following days I experienced some very powerful zazens. The breakthrough came on the afternoon of the fourth day. I was feeling sleepy and restless, but I devoted myself to the counting and breathing and went into a very peaceful state. My vision altered and this was increased by the reciting and singing of the Evening Service. I understood the power meditation can have on the making of music.

On a previous retreat I had been walking up the hill and had found a lamb which had gotten out of the field. Three of us had spent a long time running after the lamb to return it to its mother. This year, almost the exact situation was repeated but this time with Shih-fu present. He pointed at the lamb and I just walked up to it with none of the excitement of last time. I picked up the frisky animal and returned it to its place. It seemed to me a significant event, showing me that I was becoming calmer in life, more effective in my day to day being.

In the few days that have followed the retreat, the words of Shih-fu have been echoing around me. At the time, I wondered if I could possibly remember any of it, but it warms me to know that they are somewhere deep inside me. The metaphor of the glass mountains sums this retreat up for me. It was no easy ride, I was constantly confronted by my aversion to concentrate and by my own mind which has had so much invested in past pain and future hopes. It showed me how I trade my 'here and now' in favour of these false gods. The retreat gave me a valuable lesson in dedication – but this dedication must be both strictly disciplined and compassionately relaxed.

Comment
Facing the anxieties that are the products of past pain constitutes a fearsome barrier. Patience before the wall is hard to maintain. The will to continue is threatened. It seems like masochism. Actually this discipline is a kindness to oneself, because, as the mind becomes calmer, insights emerge. It becomes possible to do the obvious and no more – returning a lost lamb to its field.

3. *Therapist and linguist. Female*

I have driven to sit on the edge of a peaceful lake surrounded by trees and daffodils. The sun is warm, and sparkles brightly on the water. A glorious spring day has arisen 'out of the blue' and I am happy that Shih-fu will experience this, after the cold and wet conditions that prevailed during the retreat.

I am aware of wanting to write something good, to please Shih-fu so that he will think of me, remember my name, recall my face. But then I remember the verse from *Calming the Mind:*

> Using speech
> or written words
> To gain the praise of others
> Is something most repulsive.

The first thing that impressed me was the great respect that Ch'an has for both Earth and Heaven. By Earth I mean the practical, pragmatic, the concrete, the detail. No room was left for confusion in any area of practical explanation or instruction concerning meditation, prostration, services, exercises, or walking. I find this concern for clarity, precision and detail a very special form of love and care for sentient beings. I so often feel lost and clumsy when I am introduced to something new in an off-hand or careless manner. I feel I should know without being told, and end up feeling inadequate and discouraged. With Shih-fu and his excellent 'team' I did not feel unintelligent or clumsy. So I thank the Master and his Method for this earthy, practical compassion.

Then there was Heaven. The Master's description of Enlightenment and its different levels, brought Heaven down to Earth, it demystified the ineffable and put it in the realms of the possible, allowing me to see clearly, at least intellectually, what the supreme state must be like; and that is a great service in an area which to me has often seemed shrouded in deliberate obscurantism.

During the retreat I enjoyed watching my response to the difficulties inherent in such a crowded environment, the automatic concern that the self should be all right – I wanted a comfortable bed space, a 'good' seat at the table, a 'good' spot for sitting, generous portions of food, work that I liked. I stood back and tried to let go of these preoccupations, old graspings which persist in my personality despite much 'growth work' and meditation over a period of fourteen years or so. I noticed my dislike of hard work and was dismayed at being given the garden to dig, worried that I'd hurt my back and not be able to sit well. Interestingly at the point where I began to enjoy the digging, I was told to stop as we needed to exercise on the plot I was working on.

I loved burning the rubbish in the garden, making a leaping, roaring blaze. The extent to which I rejoice in these external fires, shows me how much I need to continue cultivating the inner fires of inspiration, warmth, compassion in my own being. Sheng Yen reminded me that Ch'an is a very warm practice and so it answers this need in me. Now, sitting by my calm still lake, I am aware of a warm glow in body and mind which the six days' intensive sitting have generated.

In meditation I started with simple wall-gazing and it didn't feel quite right. In interview Sheng Yen told me that after fourteen years of various Buddhist practices, I should use this retreat to do something more demanding. So I went off with the koan 'Who am I?', a question which has again become relevant in my life when at fifty most of my old roles and functions have slipped or been torn away and I have once again to recreate my life and my self anew. This koan soon began to feel like a frail boat tossed on an ocean of energy that was too strong for it; the question seemed almost an irrelevance in such a strong sea. I told this to Sheng Yen in the second interview and he understood, saying I needed to work on something stronger. He suggested 'What is Mu?'. This question, familiar, I imagine, to many Ch'an practitioners, was quite new to me, and stimulating. I enjoyed working with it and after half a dozen sittings began to feel a strong surge of energy around the heart, warmth and loving feelings began to flow. Ah I thought. This must be it. What is Mu? 'Mu is love'.

I got myself an early interview. Shih-fu's face was stern, rebuking perhaps, as he said very firmly 'No'. Why had I been rushing, so anxious to get an answer? He came up with an image of what I had done, I had brought him 'a frozen fruit'. I have a clear image in my mind of having taken to him a small raspberry, or strawberry, red, but still icy from the freezer, glistening with frost, unthawed love. Premature love. Premature Mu. Sobered, a little let down, I went back to my cushion and worked more calmly for two days, deprived myself of an offered interview a day later, feeling slightly ashamed of my precipitate action, yet knowing that I had needed to follow that energy that felt like love and survive any possible rebuke from Shih-fu without feeling undermined or hurt. I had acted 'out of character' for I am normally reserved, cautious, patient – a typical Capricornian earth person, so it was a measure of my trust in Master Sheng Yen that I had allowed myself to rush in like a fool, where angels fear to tread.

The rebuke brought learning. I entered a calm plateau of strong clear meditation where I learned how my practice had often been tense and striving. I learned to soften my mind, to order it to be bright and clear. I asked 'What is Mu?' as we walked, slow or fast, out of doors, in the fields and it began to appear in the energy of walking; it was there also in the movement of the reeds on the bank of the river and in the rippling, bubbling of the waters of the stream; it glowed in the little golden straws on the ground and in the sheeps' droppings; the earth was a mosaic of shape, form, colours animated by Mu. It fired the sun and moved in the wind. I felt that Mu was perfect balance and harmony, neither too precipitate nor too sluggish. This Mu was much richer than my first experience; maybe the frozen fruit was melting a little.

I shared this Mu with Sheng Yen and there was a warm smile on his lips and in his eyes. 'It is a very good feeling, isn't it?' and, 'Ch'an is a very warm practice.'

I was aware of having broken a pattern. In past retreats I have tended to strive towards some result, which I usually achieve after four or five days' 'sitting'; it takes the form of high energy, insight, or peak experience, often accompanied by joy and lightness. These experiences feel very worthwhile at the time but they are rarely sustained for more than a couple of weeks, before the return of old vexations, daily patterns of anxiety, frustration or irritation. This time the pattern had been interrupted by Sheng Yen and instead of the excited 'peak', I had had several days of calm, strong, meditation and a feeling of equilibrium. I learned more about controlling my mind and softening it; most of the pain and agitation in my body departed after a few days; and there was the gentle but unforgettable experience of Mu, lightening up the countryside, seeing the soft glow and harmonious pattern of all created things.

A query for me about Ch'an concerns the place of the feminine. I know that Zen is part of a patriarchal, masculine tradition and I read in a recent Buddhist publication, 'Meetings with Remarkable Women', that many dedicated and gifted women practitioners in America have felt obliged to create alternative retreat centres more in keeping with feminine values and less embedded in patriarchal tradition. I am not a feminist, having equal respect for both masculine and feminine qualities and values, but I am aware, along with many others in society, that the world has lost its relationship with the feminine principles which need to be respected and restored if nature and people are to survive the coming years with integrity, balance and wholeness.

Master Sheng Yen I felt, embodied both aspects, having the rigour, discipline and intellectual clarity of the masculine principle, and a flow, flexibility and caring with regard to us as individuals, which had a warm 'maternal' quality. With my little knowledge of Ch'an, I have no idea whether this is a characteristic of the tradition, or an instance of one individual master attaining a balance and wholeness based on the strength of his own practice, experience and character.

I bow down to the Three Jewels and to the Master who travelled for fifty hours without sleep to bring Dharma and light to a little cottage that slumbered on the Welsh hills, with its candles and oil lamps waiting to welcome him.

Comment
Daffodils and sunlight are there to be loved. Not getting the right seat at table causes problems. Alone on retreat when nobody else may seem to care, wanting to be comfortable expresses a need for self-indulgence. Meeting a mind of humility, Shih-fu's rebuke brought forth the golden world. Yet, when the silence of unity contains the means, why discuss the male and the female?

4. *Industrial chemist. Senior research manager. Male.*

A few days before the retreat, when it seemed that Shi-fu would not be able to come, I was not particularly bothered. I was looking forward to seven days' practice. None the less, I was delighted to see him at Maenllwyd. After hours of near continuous travel with little sleep, he looked remarkably relaxed. This calmness, exhibited by both Shi-fu and Guo Yuen Shih, made a great impression on me several times during the retreat.

This was a difficult retreat for me, but one that has left a much more lasting impression that many 'easier' retreats. It wasn't difficult because of the sitting, although my body did ache at times. Rather it was the incessant noise of my mind and certain attitudes, particularly of self-pride, that caused me problems. The fourth day was one of the worst I have ever experienced on a retreat. Perhaps I should say, 'one of the worst days I've given myself', as all the problems were generated by my mind. During morning service I had been deeply moved by the words of the Three Refuges and by the beauty of the chant in Chinese led by Guo Yuen Shih. During the next meditation period, I felt a kind of surrendering. I felt very vulnerable. I told this to Shih-fu during interview and he seemed pleased. Then the sitting got difficult. My mind was constantly disturbed by thoughts.

I began to feel resistant to Shih-fu, rejecting of his instruction, even though, at the same time, I knew it was totally correct. Something in me was insisting on doing the retreat my way instead of his. I wanted to laugh, to walk in the countryside, to hug people, to enjoy the food. I knew these to be distractions but I nevertheless wanted to *enjoy*. Several times I wondered why I was doing this retreat. Yet at other times, maybe only a few minutes later, I was really glad to be doing it. I wanted to do nothing else, I wanted to be a monk and train with Guo Yuen Shih! The see-saw between attraction and repulsion went on all day. At bed time, I was feeling thoroughly resistant to Shih-fu. I went to bed fed-up, disillusioned. I sympathised with another participant who said she had felt angry all day. I felt that Ch'an training was a waste of time. At the same time, I was wondering if all this trauma was not just my resistant ego imagining itself threatened.

On waking to the sound of the boards clapping, I recalled a vivid dream in which I was sitting on a small wooden platform constructed part way up a high wall. A pyramid of similar platforms fanned out below me, like steps, and I had to get down to the bottom. I was proud to be sitting at the top, but worried about getting down, as the steps seemed too far apart, and I was sure to fall if I took the direct route downwards. Someone in the dream said 'Well, how do *you* think you could get down then?' I said 'I could do it this way', pointing to an alternative way slightly to the side. This was still a bit dangerous but as it seemed possible, I set off downwards. Another voice said, 'Well, it's *your* body' – meaning I had full responsibility for my own actions and their consequences. I felt very relieved by the dream. I knew I had to find my own way, to be myself, but somehow this no longer seemed to be at odds with Shih-fu's way.

During the sitting after breakfast I felt very emotional. Tears coupled with vivid images came in waves. The need to find my own way was accompanied by a desperate need for help from Shih-fu. The two were not contradictory any more. I felt love for Shih-fu and for Guo Yuen Shih, love for their calmness and tranquillity. Much of this release of emotion was triggered by an impending interview with Shih-fu, who was most unimpressed with my words and emotional state. 'It is just your ego,' he said, 'continue your practice.'

Yes, I knew my ego was the problem. I felt gratitude to him for helping me to see myself clearly and went back to practise diligently. I resolved to count breaths constantly for the remaining days of the retreat and not let any ego-generating thoughts get hold of me. For the rest of the day I did so, all through sitting, through lunch, food preparation, and washing in the stream. During the first sitting after lunch I was very tired and nearly fell over several times. I wondered whether to go for a sleep. But then the next sitting was easy, relaxed, a quiet mind, the best of the whole retreat. This was real practice. I arose from the sitting with a feeling of amazement. I began to see the depth of Shih-fu and wanted to do more practice with him. I realised that I have one main task to focus on day to day after the retreat – to calm my mind by removing attachment. That afternoon was my best ever lesson in what training is about.

How rough and unsettled my mind is when compared to these monks! I am buffeted by the thoughts and emotions they generate. All the thoughts are a consequence of my attachment to various things in my life and to memories. The day after the retreat ended, the first writing I did was to list my attachments. I have to let go my attachment to (i) career, which disturbs my mind with both desire for success and recognition and fear of failure or personal rejection, (ii) personal property, especially my home and car, in which I have a compulsion to meet the 'standard' set by my parents, (iii) security, my desire for a financial buffer to ensure my standard of living, (iv) food, my desire to eat and enjoy is only tempered by my attachments to, (v) my body, which I want to keep fit, healthy and attractive, (vi) my garden, wherein I have a strong desire to produce a beautiful place in which to relax, but attachment prevents my mind relaxing in the end result! (vii) quiet, beautiful environments, my mind being disturbed by rejection of noise, disturbance, dirt, squalor and disturbed by desire for beauty, quiet, peaceful-ness, (viii) sex, which is generated by thought, and is just a longing for the peace that is so briefly attained, (ix) self-pride, especially pride in having some experience of Buddha Dharma, (x) worst of all, attachment to the desire for peacefulness of mind, the desire itself being a constant disturbance. Much better to practise with no intent or desire.

The last day of the retreat passed easily and I felt very relaxed. Even though this was a retreat without any 'special experiences', I feel quite changed by the contact with Shih-fu and Guo Yuen Shih. Their instruction was invaluable. More than that, the experience of their presence remains within me.

Comment
Loving the master and killing the father are the struggles of self with the realities of authority. Persistence in confronting self-importance is a vital attribute on the way. How to find one's own place? How to be the true man of no dependence? Remember: letting go into the ordinary is not the same as a praiseworthy programme of abandonments.

5. *Research psychologist. Female.*

This retreat was quite unlike the others I have attended. I am not amazed by extraordinary experiences; I am not tired and excited by the intellectual stimulation; I am not trying madly to maintain clarity of mind or mindful concentration. Instead I feel quite ordinary. If anything, I am pleasantly myself, more relaxed, open and friendly. I get occasional bouts of saying to myself 'I must stay alert, I must make the most of what I have learned in this week' – but I don't go on with it.

Nothing much seems to have happened. The oddest thing was a feeling on the last day that I could not remember anything of the retreat at all. Instead of a mental list of experiences I'd had or things I'd learned, there was a great blank. At first it frightened me a little. Then I appreciated it. Clearly nothing was amiss with my memory because I could clearly recall the helpful morning teachings. No – there just was not a dramatic series of 'events' to be recalled.

The first day was terribly hard even though I knew I could cope. I spent the whole day fighting tiredness and cold. Each meditation session was a round of battling, relaxing, fighting, dozing off, waking up, hallucinating ever more wildly, fantasising, thinking about torture or other horrible forms of human suffering, passing out into half sleep and longing endlessly to put my head down or to find some warmth. I consoled myself by thinking that I would stop daily meditation from now on and that I would go home and cook a huge joint of beef. I don't normally eat meat!

Shih-fu was talking about not using the eyes and ears. In my practice of mindfulness, I had always found myself alert to sounds and sights around me and I loved the vividness. When he talked about the sensations leaving no trace this made sense but I was worried by the idea of becoming blind and deaf. Nevertheless, I began directing my attention more inwardly. It was several days before I gave in to this idea and, with increasing isolation, found that I did indeed become somewhat blind and deaf. Nothing looked substantial any more. This was both heartening and frightening.

I began to love my job and to look forward to it. I thought less about what was happening next, so I didn't look forward to anything much. When doing the job, I found it easier to feel that body and mind were not totally separate. Work, and the walking, reminded me of skiing. It was odd to find myself comparing my favourite activity in the whole world with scrubbing dirty pots and walking in a circle in a muddy field, but there was the same sensation of total involvement, commitment and flow.

One evening we had a lecture suggesting that you cannot be able and talented, know you are able and talented, and work well at Ch'an. I commented that it was precisely being able and talented which had brought me to Ch'an. When people praise my work, ideas or paintings I find it extremely uncomfortable because I am being compared and don't want to put others down. I feel embarrassed as well as pleased; yet still I crave such praise. It is this unsatisfactoriness which keeps me meditating. On a retreat like this, if you compare your progress with anyone else's, then clearly it is only in your own imagination.

On the fourth day, the thoughts came. I was surprised they took so long. I didn't know what to do. I used my usual methods for coping with them but more followed. I seemed to be using up more and more energy in just coping with the thoughts. I even found the walking unpleasant because my mind whirled. And I couldn't see any more. I had taken Shih-fu's advice and was becoming blind. Everything was less clear rather than more clear. I hated it. I hated the thoughts, the struggle, the tiredness and the blindness. There seemed to be an unreality outside myself and a fighting confusion within – yet I didn't mind because I thought I was getting somewhere. After all I was struggling with an interesting problem. When I looked within, as instructed, I found no-one there. I was succeeding in becoming somewhat blind to the environment but who was becoming blind? And who was doing the practising? I have often faced this question before but, this time, I was struck by the fact that clearly someone was making a huge effort.

I took this problem to Shih-fu. If I had any expectation, it was that he would, with some brilliant leap of logic, show me what the self was, or wasn't. He said, 'That is because you have not got rid of yourself.' 'Can I?' I asked. He answered, 'Stop making judgements of people, that is all.'

I went out stunned. This didn't seem to have anything to do with my question. It didn't propel me instantly into no-self. It was only a few moments later that I realised the horror of the fact that, almost every second, I was indeed judging people in my thoughts. Furthermore, there was no intrinsic difference between the judgements I made of myself or of others. There was, in fact, a massive structure of judging everyone. It was then obvious why this was an answer to my question. I set about dissolving these judgements. There was immediate success in that they decreased, but soon I arrived at the most intractable ones and I am still living with them day by day as I write.

As I struggled with these judgements, I got angry. All I wanted was sleep, yet I was beset by thought. I had wanted a week of profound illumination and insight – or beautiful experiences to recompense for the cold and hard work. Instead, I was becoming blind and deaf and living in a whirling confusion. I hated it. I hated the bloody, fucking wall, the cold, the discomfort, myself. I was angry with the world for looking so unreal, with John for making it possible and Shih-fu for telling us what to do. I hated everything.

That evening (day four) I went for a walk before the lecture and asked myself the question – what should I do with all this anger? The answer was obvious. I only had one chance here. I should keep on working hard and doing what Shih-fu said and if the whole week was that bad then tough! In other words, I should turn my anger into determination. I took a first sneaky look around (instead of keeping my eyes down) and felt glad that the world could be beautiful, even if it meant breaking the rules. I then went back to them.

Next day, I felt stronger. With all this anger and determination I could fight off sleep before breakfast. But then, with this success, came a feeling that I really didn't know what I was doing any more. Feeling proud of myself, I went to my interview and told Shih-fu. His response was not the difficult koan I had half expected or any other challenging directive. He simply gave me some helpful hints on posture and practice, told me I could take one session off to sleep if I needed to, and said 'Relax'.

I was kind of disappointed. I slept through one session, relaxed in a way that only showed me how tense I had been, and suddenly everything improved. After the next walk, Shih-fu told us we could look around. It was wonderful – a gift of sight; a fantastic clarity for a few moments. I wasn't surprised that it was short-lived but it did wonders in encouraging me.

The evening lecture was brilliant. Shih-fu managed to combine difficult ideas about the glass mountain with comprehensible guidelines. He made it seem less like fighting for attainment. From then on my meditation was different. I had many sessions in which I could relax, some in which everything seemed to flow, others which went incredibly fast. I saw many differences between sessions and between different times of day. No longer did the whole thing seem like a desperate fight against thoughts or sleep. There were some moments of emptiness. There was some peace.

I have learned how much I haven't learned. Instead of counting my accomplishments at the end of the retreat, I feel as though I have unlearned much. For the first time, I don't find the idea of the glass mountain frightening. It doesn't seem appalling to me, as it once did, that you can climb and climb and work so hard and then fall right back to the very bottom. It seems all right. If that's how it is, there is nothing to do but keep on climbing – and this retreat has been a chance to do that.

I learned why I came. I love the opportunity to get away – not from my very nice life – but from making choices, the real or imagined consequences of my own actions, my personality (developed by talking at people all the time), my watch and my filofax. I loved the isolation. Once I'd learned not to talk to anyone at all it was wonderfully freeing. Other people began to seem like ghosts.

My interviews with Shih-fu were surprising. Although they were all very short, he somehow managed, in a most down-to-earth way, to give me advice which helped me immediately and directly with my practice – and took me down a peg or two.

Comment
In judging the qualities of self and others the mind is torn between hidden arrogance and the pain of needing approval. Seeking to excel and wishing to be ordinary are neither particularly praiseworthy. Being stunned by a master may make for an angry ego. Nothing is especially important, least of all oneself. How to let it all go is indeed the tricky question. In the mountains one may learn what the task in the market-place is.

6. *Medical practitioner. Female.*

I saw the advertisement for the Ch'an retreat, at a time when I felt in need of a challenge. This seemed to be the opportunity I was looking for and so I applied, with some anxiety that I might be setting myself too severe a task. When I heard that Shih-fu was unable to come to England I was disappointed but relieved. I am now very pleased that he was able to come and I appreciate the effort that he must have made to travel so far.

I found the retreat hard. The method was difficult for me to understand, and I had to cast away many preconceived ideas. It took me a while to develop faith and obey Shih-fu's instructions. His talks were helpful and, as my mind began to calm, I felt his words come in to my meditation and this helped to settle me.

I was expecting something to happen. Nothing did. When Shih-fu told us to start seeing and hearing out in the field, I lay down and looked at the sky. I felt I was part of the sky and the sky part of me. It lasted a few seconds. Previously I would have thought, 'How wonderful, this is what unity is all about.' I was surprised that I was not disappointed when the feeling went. I realised that it was only an illusion. It dawned on me that a lot of what I have been seeing and hoping for is illusory. When I sat in the chair at tea time I realised that there was nothing to seek and nothing to find. I understood a lot of my previous illusions and attachments and felt a freedom and peace. My meditation became easier after that, but I have a long way to go before I can clear my mind of thoughts.

My deepest gratitude!

Comment
So, there is nothing to seek and nothing to find, yet such a long way still to go. How true. An opening to insight is like a match suddenly sparkling in the sunlight.

7. Social anthropologist. Male

My experiences of sitting resembled in many ways those of previous retreats. At first I was delighted to sit and blissful moments appeared, but quickly fatigue and scattered thoughts emerged and the struggle was on. The endeavour to overcome severe drowsiness and to get beyond scattered thought was very taxing especially since, as time wore on, I began to experience mild to severe backache.

Before the backache began, I found myself wrestling with thoughts about my current life situation, its general unsatisfactoriness, my seeming helplessness to change it and my deeply neurotic desire to please everyone. Depressing as these thoughts were, the calming effect of meditation soon released me from the worst feelings engendered by them and periods of blissful quiet appeared. At some such times, I felt as if I was floating on a platform above the valley; that the wall in front of me was insubstantial; I felt in contact through it and beyond it with the rolling spaces of the hills and valleys and further limitless spaces beyond them. While I was perfectly aware of the continuing innate solidity of the wall, I felt in touch with the flowing emptiness of all forms and obstacles – as if, even in a prison, a freedom could be felt and known. The trouble with the backache was that it focussed attention once more upon myself, the need for comfort, disappointment and irritation and gave rise to a growing anger which none the less powered me into resolute sitting.

At my first interview, I told Shih-fu how my mind was for ever seeking explanations, especially since, as a scientist, the need to explain had been the chief education of my mind. Shi-fu said that, for me, the most useful path was silence. I returned to sit fortified with this thought which gradually produced a feeling of stability and stillness broken, however, by repeated mind wandering and vivid dreamlike images.

As my mind became quieter, I decided to tell Shih-fu of those rare experiences of emptiness which have appeared as if by grace several times in my life and which I have been reluctant to share with anyone because of their incomprehensible nature. At interview, I gave him a straightforward account of one recent event that had followed a Western Zen retreat at the Maenllwyd. I had been down the lane on the point of departure and had returned to a gate that I had mistakenly left open, to close it. Suddenly, I saw two red kites wheeling overhead in the frost-clear air of the sunny winter day. Red kites I had never seen near Pant-y-dwr before, so I exclaimed to myself 'Oh, look at that!' I was thrilled to see them. As I gazed at the birds, my mind suddenly fell empty, I was no longer present within 'my' experiencing. There was only the landscape and the wheeling birds, a sense of joy and wonder. The experience lasted perhaps twenty minutes and I was able to feel it fading as thought reappeared and 'I returned to myself'. The experience was a re-awakening, a joy to have found it again; that paradoxical ordinariness in which the absence of self reveals the blissful wonder of the mere presence of the world

I asked Shih-fu what, from the point of view of Ch'an, was the meaning of these experiences. He told me it was 'seeing the nature'. I was overjoyed to receive his confirmation of what I had suspected but never been able to test in a direct meeting with a Master. Shih-fu also said that, from what he knew of me, he had already understood that I had had such experiences. He then said 'Congratulations' and told me to make three prostrations before him. While I was joyous and felt a great freedom, I also perceived immediately the responsibilities that this recognition implied for me. I also felt bewildered, because what had congratulations to do with simply experiencing the most basic nature of 'myself'? I felt an odd shyness for, while I was happy at Shih-fu's response, I didn't want anyone else to know. In sharing with others, minefields of potential miscommunication loomed before me. After this meeting, the sitting sessions ran smoothly and clearly with a stillness of a mirror-like quality.

Throughout the retreat, I was inspired by Shih-fu's teachings and his essentially simple yet compelling presence which varied from a companionable playfulness to an air of authority that fully transmitted the strength of the tradition. I felt immensely grateful for his spiritual friendship and deeply aware of the karma-laden difficulties of my ordinary life that I would now have to work even harder to transcend. The key-words of the brief early morning talks given under the stars in the chill air were especially striking, for they defined a Way of Being that had all the depth of Shih-fu's own authenticity.

One afternoon, we did a session of prostrations carefully explained by Shih-fu. I experienced profound repentance, not only for immediate things but for the long perspective of inadequacy in my life. As the tears poured down my face, it seemed as if repentance must be endless. Oceans of karma from past generations seemed to sweep through me. It was as if this repentance was a beginning of atonement for previous lifetimes as well as for this one. This depth of feeling gradually changed into one of relief and gratitude towards the Dharma.

Comment
Congratulations create an even greater risk. Never is the need for practice in the way more essential. Dreams of self-pride and the illusions of attainment lurk in every shadow. No wonder prostrations are worthily to be done.

8. *Management consultant. Male.*

Sleepiness and pain from recent bruising in my chest, made the first two days difficult. I used Shikantaza most of the time, which was probably mistaken because I was poorly focused. I confess that I was anxious to be using a more 'advanced' practice than watching the breath.

On the third day, I was calmer and asked for a hua-t'ou. Shih-fu suggested 'Mu'. I was delighted to have the opportunity to work on this, but unfortunately I had the wrong idea and started to ponder the story of the Dog and Buddha Nature. In the next interview, Shih-fu cleared up the problem and taught me how to investigate the question.

By the end of day three, sitting was becoming extremely painful. This was cured by adopting a different position and sitting became quite comfortable. One day I did the timing, and created a lot of mental distraction for myself around the job for I felt it increased my importance as a 'senior' student on the retreat.

On the fifth day, I became mildly anxious lest I might not solve 'Mu' in the time available, and I worked at it too intensely. One of my main vexations at all times was spiritual pride – 'I'm one of the best students.' I was surreptitiously and competitively checking other people's progress from whatever signs available. Simultaneously, I was monitoring my own progress in minute detail. This was so deeply ingrained that I was not aware of it until near the end of the retreat.

At one point, my mind scattered in a wave of anxiety and disappointment at the thought that I would not finish 'Mu' before the retreat was over. By counting the breath I was able to re-establish attention and so return to Mu. At the time, this felt like quite an accomplishment!

Before going to sleep on the last night, my mind began to disintegrate, as each thought arose it fell away unconnected to other thoughts. 'I' almost disappeared, but not quite, and the mind flew back together again at the first opportunity.

On the final morning, Shih-fu gave further instructions on posture, breathing, and on maintaining a low centre of gravity. Following his advice led me to a much greater freedom in meditation. Yet here, there was a tendency to monitor the process, and to prompt myself with helpful hints. Much of this was subtle, not so much a thought as a kind of intensity. I tended to get excited as meditation deepened, and I found myself commentating on the process with thoughts such as 'Buddha now being born' and 'The lotus is opening'. All this foolishness is quite amusing in retrospect. Although the 'observer' still watched the 'observed', these were the clearest and most wholesome meditations of the week.

Five minutes before the final bell, 'Mu' relaxed and I was flooded with a warm feeling of fulfilment, which could be described as Dharma Food. I gave up grasping and grudging and for a short time was without doubt. Within two minutes, however, the thought arose 'But no kensho?', and so the 'hair's breadth' appeared and Buddha mind was lost, but I still felt happy and deeply grateful.

Comment
Diligence makes for a good pupil. Yet does following the way obtain the approval of the master? When not achieving is the essence of the matter the need to achieve betrays basic insecurity. Yet, how to work where this personality is undoubtedly one's own. Pursue the method until the need is seen right through. Is this splitting the hair's breadth?

9. *Medical herbalist. Male*

I have been drawn to Zen ever since I first came across books on the subject while studying for a degree in Philosophy eighteen years ago. I was unable to find any teacher, and after initial attempts at practising alone with only books for guidance, I came to a dead end. Like many of my generation, I investigated a wide range of religious and mystical traditions. Unlike many, I was never attracted to the idea of finding a 'guru', that is a person who would solve all my doubts for me in return for my unquestioning devotion. I was seeking direct experiential knowledge and, ultimately, wisdom. I finally realised that only the Mahayana Buddhist tradition met my criteria. On 1st January 1980, I took refuge formally at a Tibetan Dharma Centre in Bristol.

In the years that followed, I continued to study Buddhism. I went to various centres in the Tibetan tradition, as these were the only ones in my area. Still, I found myself truly moved only by the literature of Ch'an and Zen. I was tormented by the realisation that one of the principal tenets of Ch'an is that development cannot come about from reading books, and yet they were the only teachers I had! In 1988, I heard of the Western Zen retreats run by John Crook. I went to one, and benefited enormously. Around January of this year, John sent me details of the retreat to be directed by Shih-fu. I booked immediately, and for many weeks felt a great feeling of anticipation. A few days before the retreat was due to begin, John phoned to tell me that Shih-fu was unable to come. I naturally felt very disappointed. Once more it seemed that I was not destined to receive instruction from a Master. Strangely, on my drive to Wales, I kept thinking to myself 'Maybe Master Sheng Yen *will* come.' My rational mind told me that this was nonsense. When I arrived and learned that indeed Shih-fu was coming, I had a feeling that this event was going to be very important in my life.

Despite such an auspicious beginning, the first day of the retreat was horrific. I slept badly the preceding night, and was very tired. The hours dragged by. All I could think of was leaving. I told myself that only a mad man would subject himself to an eighteen hour day of almost constant sitting in meditation. I felt miserable, and the prospect of six more days of the same filled me with terror and dread. Yet, somewhere, a small voice told me that this was just 'monkey-mind' at work; that I'd known the first day or two would be hard; that if I left now I would be throwing away an opportunity that would probably never be available again; that giving up now would make a nonsense of my profoundest intentions, and be an unforgiveable neglect of my vows as a Buddhist, and finally, an insult to Shih-fu, who had overcome enormous obstacles to be with us in Wales. I stayed.

The second day was much better, and I began to settle into the routine of the retreat. Surprisingly, I had very little physical discomfort. My practice was not particularly good, but at least my negative feelings had subsided.

The third day started well enough, but, by mid-morning, I was in a fury with myself. Despite my most ardent intention, I was unable to still my mind for even an instant. In despair, I sought an interview with Shih-fu. He told me that being angry with myself was useless. I should relax. He recommended that I should itemise my thoughts – pen them up like the sheep in the fields around us; also, that I should lower my centre of gravity from my head to my seat. I did as Shih-fu suggested and there was much improvement. I saw how essentially banal, repetitive and absurd most of my thoughts were, and gradually they became less troublesome. They never ceased entirely but this came to matter less. The rest of the retreat passed well for me. I no longer sought 'wu'/ 'kensho' experiences. I had some very good sittings, some very indifferent ones. But quietly, gradually, Shih-fu's teachings were taking root. I had the feeling that a true transmission was taking place, and although the fruits of this transmission might take years, even lifetimes, to fully ripen, I had at last been given a true foundation for practice.

I am still amazed that of all the seekers and practitioners in this country and indeed in Europe who would have seized this opportunity, I am one of the few who has had the benefit of contact with a living Ch'an Master. Such rare good fortune makes me realise that only by diligent and continued practice can I begin to do justice to the privilege I have enjoyed. The simple profound teachings that Shih-fu gave us are not only a solid basis for meditation practice, but also a way for my everyday life. I shall carefully and diligently work to nurture Ch'an.

An evening dream – everything an illusion;
I cannot explain one part of what I saw.
Yet in the dream it seemed truth stood before my eyes.
This morning, awake, is it not the same dream?

Ryokan

Comment
The capacity to endure ends in gratitude. Patience gives way to calm. Yet, where now is the Master?

3 SHIH-FU IN LONDON: APRIL 1989

AFTER OUR retreat in Wales, I drove Shih-fu and Guo Yuen Shih to London to see something of the great city before their return to New York. It was an extraordinary privilege to be in close company with Shih-fu for these few days. The period after a retreat tends to be a time of important insights and to spend that time with a Ch'an master is a special opportunity. Needless to say, it was a time I shall always remember. The characteristic of Shih-fu that stands out most clearly in my mind is his deliberate cultivation of simplicity and directness. This may sometimes have the appearance of a certain remoteness but, as I became familiar with it, I saw it increasingly as demonstrating a door to joy and insight. The following autobiographical interview and brief stories try to show what I mean. They seem important because simple events can have telling consequences through the insights they afford. Each story is best read separately.

The autobiographical interview was part of a long conversation with Shih-fu which took place in my children's flat in Great Russell Street. Guo Yuen Shih and Lai Shun Yuan acted as interpreters and we ranged over many points of the Dharma. Shih-fu agreed that such an interview might be a useful part of this book and he has allowed me subsequently to insert into it stories of his life which I have picked up from other sources, particularly an account of his life to be found in *Getting the Buddha Mind*.

AUTOBIOGRAPHICAL INTERVIEW

I was born into a poor family of farmers who lived in the countryside outside Shanghai. My father was a peasant who did not own land but worked in the rice fields of others. He was a kind man and I never saw him angry. My parents were both intelligent but my father said very little. My mother was more forthcoming than he was. I had three brothers and two sisters. None of them was interested in becoming a monk or a nun and my brothers remained on the land.

When I was a small child, I was very stupid. At three years old I couldn't even walk. At four I had not begun to talk. Only when I was six did I start talking. And, even then, I could neither tell left from right nor tell the time. I went to primary school when I was eight and was in my fourth year when the war between Japan and China started. Because of the war I had to stop my schooling when I was twelve.

When I was seven, the Master who was to become my first teacher was searching for a disciple. He asked the Buddha where he should look and the Buddha told him to go to the source of the Yangtze River. He had to go and look in that direction. One of this man's followers, a lay disciple, happened to be a neighbour of my family. One day, when it was pouring with rain, he was walking by and stopped in front of our house. The rain was so appalling that he came into our house to escape the downpour. As he was talking to my mother he noticed that a small boy was in the room. It was me. He asked my mother whether it would be all right if this little boy became a monk. My mother said 'Oh! That is his own choice. It's his business. If he likes to do it then that's fine by me.' So the man asked me if I would like to be a monk – but I did not know what a monk was!

Anyway, he wrote down my name and my birthdate and took them to the Master who put them up in front of the Buddha image and left them there for half a year. After that time, the Master asked if this boy was the correct choice. The

Buddha said yes. In some Chinese temples the sticks of the I Ching are used to choose disciples; the method whereby I was chosen was very unusual.

The name of this Master was Lun-wei. He shaved my head when I joined him for studies at the age of thirteen. I was with him for five years. He was monk in the Lin-chi tradition. None of us young monks had any idea of the nature of Ch'an training and we received no adequate instruction. We simply followed the rigorous discipline of monks, washing clothes, working in the fields and performing daily services. I had to memorise sutras and at this I proved singularly inept. My Master told me that my karmic obstructions were very heavy and made me prostrate endlessly to Kuan Yin. I prostrated five hundred times every night and again in the morning before the other monks were up. After three months, I felt a curiously refreshing experience. My mind became clear and I no longer found memorisation a problem. Even today, I believe Kuan Yin came to my aid, for I was really very dull of mind until that time.

None of us knew anything of the history of Buddhism either in China or India. Indeed few Chinese had an understanding of the Dharma or much respect for it. The religion was still in severe decline and the monasteries provided little in the way of an appropriate education. Training was intended to be through daily experience. I felt the value of the teachings and a sadness that so few venerated them. I vowed to study so that I might bring them to others. Due to the spread of Communism, we moved into Shanghai where we made ends meet by performing the rituals for the dead. I ran away from my monastery to study at a school in the city where young monks could obtain some formal instruction. My master eventually approved of this move.

The seminary had been founded by the great reformer Master T'ai-hsu (1889–1947) who, together with Master Hsu-yun (1840–1959), was responsible for the revival of Chinese Buddhism in the early part of this century. T'ai-hsu was influenced by a line of thought from the great Master Ou-i Chih-hsu (1599–1655).[1] This teacher had disapproved of sectarianism and insisted that there was really only one tradition with varying aspects. He placed equal emphasis on the eight schools; Hua-yen, T'ien-t'ai, Ch'an, Wei-shih (Mind Only), Vinaya, Chung-kuan (Madhyamaka), Ching-tu (Pure Land) and Tantra. He taught that when one looked inward at the content of the deluded mind one discovered the true 'mind of thusness' considered to be the foundation of the 'Mind Only' doctrine of the Vijnanavada school. When one looks outward, one experiences the transformation of this basic consciousness into the everyday functional mind.

I studied history and the T'ien-t'ai, Hua yen, Wei-shih and Vinaya teachings. There was also an emphasis on physical exercises (Tai-chi) and boxing. Ritual repentance was much stressed. We practised meditation but without adequate instruction. I simply did not know what I was supposed to be doing. I puzzled over this so much that I entertained many doubts and questions about meditation. We were told that only when 'the bottom fell out of the barrel' were we allowed to see the master. Unfortunately, nobody seemed to know what this meant and my doubts remained unresolved.

The war years were very bad and I had to be a soldier from the age of eighteen until I was twenty-eight. When the Kuomintang came to Taiwan I was in the army and came with them. In the years between 1949 and 1959 there was no way in which I could leave the army. In the end I became a monk again, lived in a temple in Taiwan and edited the magazine *Humanity*. I went back into training and attended retreats. The doubts persisted. I was constantly wondering what Enlightenment or Buddhahood was. There were so many contradictions in the teachings that I could make no sense of them; the deeper I looked, the worse it became.

When I was twenty-eight I had a profound experience of dropping the mind. It happened like this. I had been prac-tising a lot and had had some small experiences, yet all these puzzles kept running through my head. I went on retreat in a temple in southern Taiwan where a famous monk, Ling-yuan (1902–1988), was visiting. One night, he and I were sharing the same sleeping platform and, seeing that he was meditating, I sat with him. My doubts were going round and round in my head, one leading to another; they were all about the nature of vexations, life and death. After some hours, between ten and midnight, these worries became intolerable. I asked the monk whether I could ask him a question. He said yes. When I started, all the questions gushed out in a sudden flow. They poured out of my mouth like water. It went on and on for two to three hours. I felt I needed answers from this monk who seemed so free and easy in himself. All he did was to listen. He said nothing or simply asked 'Any more?' It was very strange. I had started with one question and suddenly there was this endless flow. It was the 'great ball of doubt'. After a long time the monk suddenly sighed, lifted his hand and struck the bed hard. 'Put it down,' he said. Suddenly my mind seemed to snap. I was pouring with sweat and felt a great weight being suddenly lifted from me. There was nothing there. It seemed that there was no problem anywhere in the world. Everything had gone. We simply went on sitting – not saying a word. I was extremely happy. The next day the whole world was fresh as if I were seeing it for the first time.

In the practice of meditation, it is not possible to 'see the nature' through willing or intending it. It is essential to bring positive causal conditions together so that one can practise under the instruction of someone who has sufficient insight to be a guide for you. Not any teacher will do. You have to let go into purposeless practice. If there is purpose the discriminating mind is active and the ego is present. You have to work hard on your method. It is neither a matter of waiting nor of not-waiting.

When at last I had left the army, I found a certain Master Tung-ch'u (1907–1977), who I sensed to be an extraordinary individual. He neither lectured nor gave instructions on practice. Yet, seeking neither fame nor followers, he was widely respected. He was an heir to both the Lin-chi and the Ts'ao-tung lineages. His way of speaking was startling and could affect people deeply. My stay with him was rough indeed. He treated me much as Marpa the great Tibetan had treated Milarepa. He would tell me to move into one room, and then into another – and then back again at once. He told me to seal off a door in a wall and open another. Although we used a gas stove, I had to fetch logs from high up in the hills. I never got the wood the right size; it was always too large or too small. Similarly, when I sat, he would say 'You cannot become a Buddha by sitting. Mirrors are not made by polishing bricks.' I was then ordered to do prostrations. After several days he would say 'This is nothing but a dog eating shit. Go and read the sutras.' So I would read for a couple of weeks. Then he would say 'The Patriarchs thought the sutras only good for cleaning sores. Go and write an essay.' When I had done it, he would tear it up saying 'These are only stolen ideas. Using your original wisdom say something!' Whatever I did was wrong, even when I had done exactly what he had told me to do. This harsh teaching was actually very compassionate. Without him, I would not have realised much. His message was that one had to become self-reliant in the practice. After two years, I decided to go into solitary retreat in the mountains. I told him I had vowed to practise hard so as to not fail the Dharma. 'You are wrong,' he said. 'What is this Dharma? What is Buddhism? The important thing is not to fail yourself!'

I found a remote spot and did a solitary retreat for six years. I lived in a small hut which looked out onto a cliff. There was a small courtyard and, although I always remained within it, I never felt closed in. All the time I felt calm and settled as if I had come home. I ate one meal a day of wild potato leaves which I planted myself. Originally I only intended to do three years. During the first one, I spent most of the time doing repentance prostrations. The second year I spent in meditation and reading sutras. The third was the same. I then realised there was simply not time enough to complete my project, so I continued. I began to read and study. I also started to do research and to write. I spent half my time meditating and half in study. After six years, I had written several books and learned to read Japanese. I then stopped my retreat and went to Japan for further studies, taking a Doctorate in Literature at Rissho University in Tokyo. I also went on retreats, especially with Bantersugu Roshi, a disciple of Sogaku Harada Roshi. I attended winter-long retreats at his temple in the harsh environment of Hokuliku in northern Japan. He was particularly scathing about my learning and studying at university. I was thinking of going to the USA and, before I left Japan I discussed this with the Roshi. I complained that I did not know English. He said 'Do you think Zen is taught by words? Why worry about words?'

Nowadays, I am very busy. I have an institute to direct in Taiwan, a monastic temple to organise and another institute in New York. I divide my time between Taiwan and New York. I have also taught Buddhist philosophy in the Soo Chow University in Taipei. I usually teach Hua yen and T'ien-t'ai but, nowadays, I am also teaching Madhyamaka. In my institute, the Institute of Chung Hwa Buddhist Culture, I have also taught comparative religion. I use texts and notes from which to provide instruction in the usual way when teaching academically. In giving Ch'an teachings at retreats, however, everything that is said arises spontaneously. I also look after a journal, *The Chung Hwa Buddhist Journal*, and write articles for it. So I keep up my research in Buddhism.

At my institute, we have a graduate school in Buddhist Culture consisting of about twenty-five students at any one time. It is a three year course and each year we have five or more students entering school. They mostly have very good degrees from elsewhere. We also teach the Pali and Tibetan languages as well as instruction in Chinese.

The students are also taught to meditate and to participate in retreats together with the monks and nuns of the temple. Some lay practitioners who are my disciples also come. There are about thirty monks and nuns at the monastery. All are young – in their twenties and thirties. I am the only old monk! Now we are planning a new monastery on a beautiful mountain outside Taipei city. It is near the sea and will eventually hold some three hundred people but will take about ten years to complete.

When I teach monks and nuns the emphasis is different from my approach in teaching lay people. We focus particularly on the Vinaya – that is to say the way to behave in being a monk. The main focus is on being non-dependent, on being 'a lamp unto oneself'. This is very much 'guarding the one' in the way we talked about during our retreat in Wales.

The monk or nun needs to internalise new ways of experiencing in order to be a true member of the Sangha.

In everyday life it is important to maintain awareness. Yet, if one has a complex task to do, it is not always possible to avoid a divided mind. If it is not allowed to scatter there is no harm. One should know the mind is divided in order to do a particular task better. Afterwards one should relax into a unified state. If you are looking out of the window – you just look out of the window. If you are driving the car, you just do it. It's not a matter of enjoying or not enjoying. You just notice what is happening without dependence on the quality of feeling.

The training of monks and nuns today is more difficult than it used to be. This is because young people today grow up in a culture in which they are taught to be very independent in the individualistic sense. When I was young this was not so. We respected authority in a less questioning manner. Today it is necessary for the teacher to meet argument with argument. Egotistical and highly intelligent students want to know Why? What? and Wherefore? Yet this can be very positive and creative when the intelligence is properly engaged. The important thing is for the young trainees to develop a different lifestyle and to change the quality of the mind. They need to practise, read the biographies of the Patriarchs and then choose what kind of monk or nun they wish to be. Some may teach, some may do work as professional helpers, some become apprentice practitioners, some help run the temple. It depends on their abilities and talents. Actually, the main principle for a modern monk or nun is not to escape society but to find out how to contribute to it. The first thing is to offer yourself to the Three Jewels and then to find out how to help sentient beings.

ENCOUNTERS

On the Road to Town

We left Oxford and headed east on the main road to the big city. As I drove, I remarked to Shih-fu that I was not entirely sure of the route. London was full of one-way streets, traffic jams, post-rush hour congestion, and roadworks. I was afraid we might get off the streets I knew and take a long time to get to our destination, my children's flat in Great Russell Street.

Shih-fu said, 'Have you driven the route before?' I told him that I had driven most of it previously but could not say that I was familiar with it.

'Well then,' said Shih-fu, 'just drive it and see what happens.'

At this I relaxed and just drove. Each roundabout and intersection posed no problem. Finding the correct lane came about without any mistakes. It became obvious which way I had to go. I drew up outside the flat at precisely the time I had predicted when we had left Oxford – barring no delays. The imagined delays had simply disappeared.

The Taxi Driver

It was a glorious sunny morning, a cloudless sky and flowers everywhere; one of those extraordinary city days when London appears like a bride dressed for a wedding. We came out into the street and hailed a taxi. We were off to the embankment to see the river Thames. As I gave the instruction to the driver I remarked, 'On a day like this it must be a joy to cruise around town.' He looked angrily at me as if I was a kind of idiot. 'You must be joking,' he said, 'heat, fumes, traffic too much for the road system. I'm sick of it and the weather makes it worse – just think I might be lying on a beach somewhere.' He looked so glum, I said no more. In the back of the taxi, Shih-fu, Guo Yuen Shih and Lai Shun Yuan were talking animatedly as we went along; theatres, Trafalgar Square with Nelson's Column, people, clothes. When we drew up beside the shining river with its elegant bridges I remembered Wordsworth's lines:[2]

> This City now doth like a garment wear
> The beauty of the morning; silent, bare,

Ships, towers, domes, theatres, and temples lie
Open unto the fields, and to the sky;
All bright and glittering in the smokeless air.

I was paying the driver when he said to me, 'We must have met before. About a month ago I took some Chinese around the city and you must have been their host, as you are today. I like the Chinese. They have a friendly quality. It's been good driving you. And, regarding what I said before. No, it's not a pleasure driving around town. It's just my job. But I am grateful to be able to do it. It might be otherwise.'

He was smiling. I didn't tell him I was sure we had never met.

The Buddhist Centre

Shih-fu wanted to buy some books for the library at the Ch'an Center in New York, so we went to a well-known Buddhist centre in the city where there is an excellent book shop. As soon as I had introduced Shih-fu formally, the young receptionist seemed to undergo some psychological transformation. His rather offhand and preoccupied manner suddenly became one of ardent genuflection as he rushed to get us tea and biscuits, sit us in the best chairs and provide us with all the comforts of an honorific occasion. He showed us around the premises and, when we came to the staircase, he said to me confidentially, 'With a Zen Master present should I stand aside and let him go upstairs first or should I show the way?' He was terribly anxious to get it right.

I said 'Since it is you who know the way, why not lead on?' With great relief he did so.

After we had left, I asked Shih-fu whether he had noticed the stir his presence had caused in the centre and the great anxiety to please that the younger staff had shown. How polite this was in some sense but how peculiar it felt after having just experienced a retreat.

Shih-fu said 'The difficulty in such a place is that people are often selling the Dharma – not offering it.'

Horse Shit

We were walking in Parliament Square admiring the Palace of Westminster and the looming complex of the abbey buildings. A great swirl of traffic was thundering around the square, which is a main city thoroughfare. Huge lorries, delivery vans, taxis, government limousines, elegant cars of the yuppie generation and the scruffy ones of the lesser orders all poured around and around in an endless procession. Suddenly, in amongst the turning wheels, I noticed a pile of horse dung quite undisturbed by all the movement. It seemed incredible that a living horse should have passed that way so recently in such traffic and left so clear a testimony to its presence. I experienced the glimmering of a Zen paradox.

Turning to Shih-fu, I drew his attention to the unlikely pile saying, 'Shih-fu. Look! Here's a pile of horse shit – but where's the horse?'

Shih-fu looked at it and said, 'What need have we of the horse?'

NOTES

---

1. For details of this thinker and others of more recent times see: Sheng Yen, (In press) 'Four Great Thinkers of Modern Chinese Buddhism'. In: W. H. Fu and S. A. Wawrytko (eds) (In press) *Buddhist Ethics and Modern Society* (Greenwood Press Inc., USA Westport CT).
2. William Wordsworth, 'Upon Westminster Bridge'. See: Quiller-Couch, Sir A. *The Oxford Book of English Verse*, (Oxford, Clarendon).

FURTHER READING

Works in English by Master Sheng-yen

Faith in Mind: A Guide to Ch'an Practice (New York, Dharma Drum Publications, 1987).
Getting the Buddha Mind (New York, Dharma Drum Publications, 1982).
The Poetry of Enlightenment: Poems by Ancient Ch'an Masters (New York, Dharma Publications, 1987).

Selected Titles

Chang Chung-Yuan, *Creativity and Taoism* (London, Harper, 1970).
Crooke, J. H., *The Evolution of Human Consciousness* (Oxford University Press, 1980).
Crook, J. H. and D. Fontana (eds), *Space in Mind: East-West Psychology and Contemporary Buddhism* (Shaftesbury, Element Books, 1990).
Fields, R., *How the Swans Came to the Lake: A Narrative History of Buddhism in America* (Boston/London, Shambhala, 1986).
Harding, D. E., *On Having No Head: The Rediscovery of the Obvious* (London, Arcana, 1986).
Kapleau, P., *The Three Pillars of Zen* (Boston, Beacon, 1965).
Kapleau, P., *Zen: Dawn in the West* (London, Rider, 1980).
Kennet, J., *Selling Water by the River* (New York, Vintage, 1975).
Kosho Uchiyama Roshi, *Approach to Zen* (Tokyo, Japan Publications Inc., 1973).

Kraft, K. (ed.), *Zen: Tradition and Transition* (London, Rider, 1988).

Leggett, T. *Zen and the Ways* (London, RKP, 1978).

Luk, C., *Chan and Zen Teaching*, 1st series (London, Rider, 1960).

Luk, C., *Empty Cloud: The Autobiography of the Chinese Zen Master Xu Yun* (Shaftesbury, Element Books, 1988).

Nishiyama, K. and J. Stevens, *Dogen Zenji's Shobogenzo: The Eye and Treasury of the True Law*, Vols 1–2 (Tokyo Nakayama Shobo, 1975).

Price, A. F. and Wong Mou-lam, *The Diamond Sutra and the Sutra of Hui Neng* (Boulder, Shambhala, 1969).

Suzuki, D. T., *The Lankavatara Sutra* (London, Routledge & Kegan Paul, 1973).

Suzuki, D. T. *Studies in the Lankavatara Sutra* (London, George Routledge, 1930).

Suzuki, S., *Zen Mind. Beginners' Mind: Informal Talks on Zen Meditation and Practice* (Tokyo, Weatherhill, 1972).

Williams, P., *Mahayana Buddhism: The Doctrinal Foundations* (London, Routledge, 1989).

INDEX